THEY HELD MY HAND

How the Beatles Saved My Life

MICHAEL MISH

They Held My Hand - How The Beatles Saved My Life

Copyright © 2020 by Michael Mish

All rights reserved. No part of this publication may be reproduced, distributed, or transmitted in any form or by any means, including photocopying, recording, or other electronic or mechanical methods, without the prior written permission of the publisher, except in the case of brief quotations embodied in critical reviews and certain other noncommercial uses permitted by copyright law. For permission requests, write to the publisher, at the address below.

Vesica Media
PO Box 3477
Ashland, OR 97520
info@michaelmish.com
www.michaelmish.com

Paperback: 978-1-888311-05-1

Ebook: ISBN: 978-1-888311-04-4

Photography by: George McKay

Book design by Grzegorz Japoł, book-cover.design

Dedicated to those that give expecting nothing in return.

TABLE OF CONTENTS

Introduction 7

CHAPTER ONE
When I Was 13 – Leaving The Valley Behind 11

CHAPTER TWO
I Want To Hold Your Hand 19

CHAPTER THREE
Revolver 51

CHAPTER FOUR
Sgt. Pepper's Lonely Hearts Club Band 65

CHAPTER FIVE
The White Album 79

CHAPTER SIX
He's Leaving Home 87

CHAPTER SEVEN
The Breakup & The Break Down 105

CHAPTER EIGHT
The Individual Beatle Voices 125

CHAPTER NINE
All I Remember Is The Music 135

CHAPTER TEN
All You Need Is Love 139

Afterword 145

INTRODUCTION

I suppose there were a few of us.

Those of us whose teen-age years coincided exactly with the beginning and the end of the greatest rock group the world has ever known. We can look at each other with instant recognition. It's a wordless understanding that runs deep.

In July of 1963, my family moved from the Valley's endless Southern California flat-lands to the city. *Hollywood*. Five months later, our handsome young president with new ideas was killed. And, for the next seven years, my life and the world changed beyond my wildest imaginings.

To find out what the hell happened throughout my teenage years, I boarded a plane bound for Europe. I was 20 years old. It was July of 1970 and I was going to make sense of it all because I was confused. Very. Europe held the answers for me. I felt that putting distance between me and everything that was familiar would bring clarity where there was none. But, really, all I remembered about that time was the music. The sounds of the sixties were not merely a backdrop to those impressionable teenage years, they were also the teacher. The consoler. The comforter. Particularly, and especially, the music of The Beatles. What started out for me as a curiosity with their innocent and optimistic vitality, quickly became an obsession. Those tidily packaged musical and, ultimately, artful expressions shaped my beliefs. They injected technicolor into my monotone world. They gave my life meaning and legitimized this deep yearning that persisted in my life since childhood.

A yearning that persists to this day.

The cleverly placed, and compelling, messages in their songs awakened the critical thinker in me. Their records replaced whatever I thought I was learning in school with a broader and more elastic learning. They awakened the desire to learn on my terms. As the reader implicitly trusts the writer to be guided through a world never-before experienced, I trusted them to be transported to seeing the world through other eyes. I was nudged awake to an experience of life different from the biased notions of my family and friends — beyond the protection of Hollywood and the LA basin. Beyond the United States. Beyond all of these influences lay a different world. A world of which I knew nothing. A world I wanted to know *everything* about. I wanted to live and breathe it. Become one with it.

In Europe, my experiences would be scored with the music of the sixties. That music covered a rich assortment of musical styles. Melodies that were engaging and compelling with lyrics that were inventive and soulful. There were the sounds of Motown, The Beach Boys, The Mamas and the Papas, Buffalo Springfield, and so very many more.

And there was The Beatles. Why do The Beatles mean more to me than any other band? The answer is simple.

Because they were The Beatles.

CHAPTER ONE

WHEN I WAS 13 – LEAVING THE VALLEY BEHIND

Farewell, oh, alfalfa fields, farms with your pomegranate, walnut and fig trees. Your concord grape vines of late summer. Goodbye to the yowling cats outside my sister, Cathy's, window that would startle her out of a deep sleep. So long, love of my life, Iris Stevens. So long to those long summer bike rides after our backyard sleepovers. So long to the early Saturday morning walks along the railroad tracks near our house. Goodbye outdoor drive-in movies and nothing-to-do weekends with forever blue skies. The golden rural landscape rung by the San Gabriel and Santa Monica Mountains. My elementary school. My junior high school. My clarinet teachers. So long to all the bittersweet memories. See you all soon enough my trusted toy-gun-slinging play mates: Christopher, Steven and Billy. We were cowboys and cowboys are friends for life, even when they move to another ranch. And, my family was moving to another ranch in Hollywood.

So long boyhood.

My first semester at Le Conte Junior High, in Hollywood, felt somehow familiar. The school, built in 1921, was nestled between two Hollywood sound stages, and had been used as an exterior for a number of TV and film locations, including *Bye Bye Birdie*.

While sitting in Ms. DeJane's French class, the school bell rang Morse code for an assembly. An Assembly? In the middle of the afternoon? There was no scheduled... *Oh.*

Someone was dead. Someone important.

Students were shepherded in silence out to this great expanse of asphalt that was our Phys. Ed. track. All of us in the school were then corralled into a huge circle from one end of the track to the other. I recall clear skies. A rust-colored oak leaf danced around aimlessly on the asphalt. It surged away and then, suddenly towards me. I watched it, hypnotized. Looking up from the leaf, the teachers' faces could not conceal their shock, disbelief and terror. Their heads hung solemnly. Many of the teachers wept openly. One of the teachers actually snorted while trying to stifle his sobs.

The only thing I could think to do was to do a back-flip from one of the bleachers. The tension was so thick, I felt I just *had* to do it.

I sprung high into the air and stuck a 10-pointer right on the ground. One of the P.E. teachers, Mr. Hensley looked at me from across the asphalt field, and just shook his head. Several days later after the assassination dust had settled, that back-flip would cost me the dreaded 'swat'—a mighty singular crack of a paddle across the back side. The paddle had been expertly crafted in wood shop. It contained holes to minimize wind resistance and result in a faster swing. The impact site would only sting for a few minutes, and then it would be over, I silently repeated to myself. I was wrong. That swat sent me crashing into the wall 10-feet away. I wouldn't be able to sit for almost two weeks; the holes on the paddle were unmistakably visible as perfectly spherical white islands in a sea of red inflamed skin. I would remember that day for a long time. The day I got my first swat. And the day that changed the United States.

> *"If art is to nourish the roots of our culture, society must set the artist free to follow his vision wherever it takes him. We must never forget that art is not a form of propaganda; it is a form of truth."*
>
> *- President John F. Kennedy,*
> *Amherst College, October 26, 1963*

JFK's assassination was the end of America's innocence. The nation had seemingly only just relegated a brutal and lengthy world war to history books. I remembered all the fathers on our block in the valley bragging to their sons about the "action" they'd witnessed overseas; how many Germans or Japanese soldiers they had killed or how many of their buddies they'd lost. My dad's only 'claim to fame' was having mortar whiz by his left ear as he sprinted down the airfield, south of London. The hangers and bombers were strafed by the Luftwaffe. He'd been loading bombs onto a B–17. My dad said the shell whistled past his ears with the hum of a giant mechanical bee.

"What? He didn't kill any Germans?" My gun-slinging cowpoke friends asked chewing on a blade of grass.

My father wasn't on the front lines. I was glad he didn't kill any Germans.

At this time, our country was basking in post-WWII prosperity. Washing machines and cars hung like ornaments on the Christmas tree of the American Dream. We'd soon enough see the USA in our Chevrolets. In a heartbeat, the United States would become an elaborate sprawl of paved highways: anyone could drive anywhere, anytime. America was enjoying the global lime-light. It was *the* place to be. The good ol' US of A with its huge automobiles and post-WWII prosperity had set us all free. Our vacuum cleaners, lawn-mowers, blenders and toasters made us feel like an unstoppable force. We'd won the war. We were the unbeatable originators of American-know-how. There was no match for our technology. We could out-gun, out-fly and out-anything — anyone.

The American dream came to a screeching halt. The man on whom the nation had pinned all their hopes and dreams for a new future. He was going to make everything even better. Trips to the moon, he said. Defeat the rapidly growing threat of Communism too. He'd put Cuba in its place. In an instant, it vanished. Camelot was gone with the clap of rifle shots.

President Kennedy's assassination, on November 22, 1963, was the end of the happiest and most optimistic of times. What followed were the gray days. The darkest months of the year and the specter of a long drab winter and a grim, spiritless Christmas.

As far as I was concerned about the assassination, I couldn't really put together what had actually happened. I remember Walter Cronkite confirming the death of our president. As a 13-year old, the news seemed surreal to me. And, frankly, even now the news seems surreal to me. How can someone so young, so charismatic, just cease to exist so…*easily*?

Then. A miracle. None of us saw it coming. None of my friends. No one in my family. Something even more exciting than looking for the ground from a tucked back-flip was about to change the way I saw the world. This light at the end of the tunnel came from the most unsuspecting of places: A newly reconstructed port town with a bustling economy and a rapidly emerging pop culture – Liverpool.

On February 7, 1964, four curious boys from this other shore, with their captivating accents and quick wit, arrived on Pan American World Airways' Flight 101 at the recently renamed John F. Kennedy airport in Queens, New York, and disembarked amid a deafening wall of teenage girls screaming themselves hoarse. Then, two days later on February 9, those same young men appeared on The Ed Sullivan Show in front of 73 million Americans and, suddenly, crazily, something very *strange* happened. Everyone knew it. Even the surprise and confusion on Ed Sullivan's face, after the group's opening song, "All My Loving": "What the hell just happened?" he must have thought. Had the Earth just wobbled on its axis? It would be my guess, but I think Ed was just as shocked as the rest of the nation was.

After those glorious two minutes and four seconds, the former upbeat American innocence returned in a flash — without missing a beat. Those four boys injected joy where there was none. They were confident and exuberant. Unlike Elvis Presley and his gyrating hips and steamy looks to the camera, they were non-threatening.

They were new. And they were new to me.

This new phenomenon had a name: John, Paul, George and Ringo.

The Beatles.

I couldn't tear my eyes from the TV. More color exploded from those black and white images than I had ever seen. It was so raw and exciting. And the girls in the TV audience seemed so out of control. It was as if something supernatural had taken hold of them. They seemed, to me, to be helpless to behave any other way. They could only scream. Seeing all these girls so completely out of control, made me smile. It made me laugh. It made me want to look at my brother and sister, and mom and dad, to see how they were reacting to this. They were as spell-bound as I was. Even Frank Sinatra, in my Dad's day, hadn't stirred up so much excitement and unbridled female hormones.

Ed Sullivan did his best to control his excitement. He must have expected that his ratings just went through the roof. He knew that this group had just put him on the television broadcasting map as the uncontested leading impresario — of the world. He did his dry Ed Sullivan every-man thing, with his inimitable sloppy diction, and gave credit to the police department and whoever else;

but everyone's minds were now solely focused on the meteor that had shot through the TV screen.

In the kitchen of our family home, I recall eating the remaining spoonfuls of my tapioca pudding with a smile on my face as the meteor's embers faded in the corners of our kitchen. For the first time in my young life, I'd witnessed an historical event with my own eyes. The event was on TV. And my life had just been touched by The Fab Four.

These four fresh faces were going to walk me down the path to something new. And it had nothing to do with Walter Cronkite or the Huntley-Brinkley Report. It had to do with seeing life anew. And out of the dark depths and austerity of a post-WWII Britain, England had transformed itself into a magical place. A classy, trend-setting, cultured, modern place. But, it wasn't merely England. It was England and it was *them*.

CHAPTER TWO
I WANT TO HOLD YOUR HAND

I want to hold your hand.

Such a plaintive and pure suggestion. 'Here. I'll cross this street with you. Give me your hand. It will be alright'.

And it was.

The United States was all of a sudden diverted and distracted away from the door slamming shut on the most somber and tragic of November days. Because another door, brimming with energy and optimism, had been opened wide in early February 1964.

As the days grew longer in February and we headed for that special summer of 1964, my step lightened with the promise of something entirely new.

The Beatles asked America if they could hold our hands, and the country gave them an exuberant "Yes!". As formerly bewildered Americans, we walked with them as they discovered themselves. Leading by their example, I discovered myself too. Their bright attitudes redefined, for me, what it was to be human. What it was to be a sensitive young male. The interviews they gave to the press were eye-opening. Instead of being on their best behavior and pandering to the world's press, they were funny, playful, unorthodox, witty and often irreverent—and I loved it. They were unflappably authentic. They were special. They challenged the interviewer as much as the interviewer challenged them. I couldn't believe what I was seeing. Their behavior couldn't be simply written off as cockiness, because they were utterly charming and completely — themselves. This was the first time that the notion of "being who you actually are," even occurred to me. I wanted to be myself too and not feel the need to do and say things that would get people to like me. I wanted to be flip, witty, and self-confident too. For me, soon to be attending High School, the idea of not needing to please others was not just a revelation, it was a liberation. The Beatles' press interviews set a new benchmark for what it was to be authentic and self-possessed. (In spite of the fact that I had nothing, particularly, to be self-possessed about.)

In whatever hole of despair a 14-year-old could be in at that time, I certainly had all the symptoms. Pimples, concerns about being acceptable and a full-blown case of

PTHSSD. Pre-Traumatic High School Stress Disorder. But The Beatles pointed to a secret passageway. A way out. It was a way out that was fun, adventurous and musical. And I was jubilant about it. As a culture, it seemed to me that The Beatles were inviting Americans to join a never-before-considered social landscape — where it was OK to be free, funny, relaxed and unconventional.

During that summer of 1964, between Junior High and High School, I was still trying to get used to living in the "city" of Hollywood. No farms. No farm animals. No fruit trees and no alfalfa fields. I desperately wanted to make new friends. I desperately wanted to meet girls.

Pat, a boy who lived next door, took me to a dance at his Catholic school that summer to meet Catholic girls. Summer was the season to meet girls. I wanted to know more about girls. I felt there was no better way to move into a new community, than to know or partner with a girl. Girls seemed to be the village gate-keepers. 'Get a girl in my corner, and I'd have instant credibility as a human being and an immediate entree into the community, I thought. Being on the good side of a girl, laid out the welcome mat to all of her friends.

At the dance, the local community of Hispanics owned all the good records; they were the ones dancing. The white kids just watched. Some dared to dance with guarded abandon to this new music. If it had been the previous summer they'd have been dancing to "Sugar Shack", "Runaway" or "Surfin' USA".

And then, emerging out of a foggy clearing between undulating 13 and 14-year-olds, there it was! I craned to see it. I needed to have it. Someone flashed it, enticingly, like a shiny gold trinket as the cover reflected the glare from the lights in the gymnasium. The fabled album cover with the black and white photo of four heads eerily floating in black space with a ghostly blue cast on their faces. Their far-away stares. Those bowl haircuts. Their faces. So different from our faces. And, music, different from our music. I had to move closer to this album cover. I needed to see it up close.

There was a prescience about The Beatles. They knew, or were about to know, something we didn't. I wanted to know what it was.

Try as I might to get near the album cover, I was pushed out of the way by an out-of-control male dancer. I just wanted to hold it in my hands. Feel the cover. Look at the LP spinning hypnotically on the turntable. Everything about this sound was new and different. Surely the label on the record would look different too.

As it played, pure energy pulsated as it lit up the room like the lightning from a Tesla coil. The girls swayed uncontrollably. This sound was different than anything from Elvis or the Big Bopper. I even wondered if the grooves made on the record looked different. It was English and everything English became a fascination for me and everyone I knew. English horse-back-riding. English accents. English Leather cologne. English toffee. English cars. English girls. Hayley Mills. Aw, man. Hayley Mills. She was more than just a young and beautiful English actress. She was my dream English girlfriend.

That night, however, it wasn't meant to be. The album cover and I were not meant to get acquainted, until later. I had to wait. They made me wait.

As a 14-year-old, my sexual awakening was a clumsy affair. No guidance or words of encouragement in health class at school. And, nothing but ridiculously funny sexual jokes from my friends. But I was guided by The Beatles. That summer, and for the many years that followed, their sound underscored the flowering of a sexual and emotional awakening.

Both John and Paul experienced their mothers being taken from them as teenagers. The tenderness of that absence made its way into their songs. That intimacy, that heart, would factor prominently in my own emotional makeup. Instead of a woman being simply a person, she became a type of salvation. She became something to complete this all-together un-whole person — who was me.

The Beatles reshaped, too, what it was to be a performer. Their genteel and humble presence was demonstrated in that deep bow that concluded their every song on stage. American performers didn't do that. We must have felt like a nation privileged to witness something so brand new and kind. Really kind: That girl loves you. This boy wants you back again. Please say you'll let me hold your hand. They had captured the hearts of America and we were goners. All of us. And they were goners too. They loved how we loved them. I could just tell.

The album image for *Meet the Beatles* haunted me for months until I broke down and bought it. My paper route helped me to scrape enough money together to buy my own copy of it. Running my thumbnail along the shrink wrapping, I felt like I was opening something sacred. The smell of something mystically new came rushing out of the record's sleeve. And, there it was. The record I'd tried so vainly to feast my eyes on those many months ago at the dance. It began with the scratchy white noise and dizzying anticipation as the needle sunk into the vinyl groove. Then: "I Want To Hold Your Hand". The music made my record player sound even better. Even the record player needle sounded as if it liked their music.

I played the songs whenever I wanted. The *sound* was unlike anything I'd ever heard. John and Paul were like the Everly's but with an edge. The Beatles were like The Shirelles with heat — and Little Richard with white restraint. Side One pulled me in and didn't let go. Following "I Want to Hold Your Hand" there was the equally riveting "I Saw Her Standing There". The simple but driving productions were exciting, fresh and raw. They had the enthusiasm of Elvis' early Sun Sessions but this was different. This was from outside our country. I felt pulled into another part of the world. Their refreshing high-octane music was redefining what rock and roll was for me. The album, however, was far too short for my taste, and I wanted more. And, for the next seven years, they didn't disappoint.

Months after I'd memorized *Meet The Beatles*, I remember my friend Tony playing the three chords to Van Morrison's "Gloria" I was entranced. "Wow," I thought. "That sounds just like the record."

With that I just had to be in a band.

For me, Beatlemania was every bit as much about marveling at The Beatles' phenomenon as it was about trying to emulate them. And we came in all shapes and sizes. I was the short guy with the over-sized saxophone who occasionally doubled on electric bass. It didn't take long for me to catch on that there was power and fun in being like a Beatle. I helped form a band late in 1964. My first band. I leaned on the other members heavily to let me sing "All I've Gotta Do" from *Meet The Beatles*. It was the perfect song for me. I practiced it tirelessly in front of an imagined audience in our living room. The other band members agreed and I sang the song in our band. For a short time, I was nearly a Beatle.

There was this annual Easter break event called the Teenage Fair in Los Angeles' Hollywood Palladium. Our drummer's mother not only got our band to play at the fair, but positioned us in the highly coveted Pepsi Booth at the fair's main entrance. I have no idea how she did it. And, I didn't want to know and didn't care. I just remember a baritone sax slung over my shoulder, ridiculously too large for my frame. The Jackson's were in a booth far less visible, and during our break I remember being floored at how tight this band of brothers was and how small these kids looked with these enormous guitars in their hands. A proud father stood to the right of their small booth. He seemed to me to be intently making mental notes of every chord, every dance move, and every vocal. As my band performed, I watched Sonny Bono, on his break from the main stage with Cher, as he studied me singing the lead vocals. We covered a lot of the tunes from that *Meet The Beatles* album. I'm sure he was wondering what had become of rock and roll now that anyone could do it. Now that everyone wanted to be a Beatle. Do the bowl haircut. Learn three chords and you're in! I can even remember our band getting girls to chase us down Hollywood Blvd. We were ridiculous. Yes. That's how badly we wanted to be Beatles. I guess that's how badly the girls wanted to be fans.

Something New

1964 was a busy year for The Beatles. There was a lot of record label cross-pollinating going on between British and American Beatles releases. But, from where I stood, there looked to have been six album releases in 1964 alone in the US. By anyone's standards — wow. They were beyond prolific. *Introducing The Beatles. Meet The Beatles. The Beatles' Second Album. A Hard Day's Night. Something New.* And, (squeaking in at the end of 1964) *Beatles 65.* Just as I'd caught my breath with one album, another one was released. I was still 14-years-old at that time and the energy of these recordings instilled in me a hope and anticipation for my future. With "I'll Be Back" and "I'll Follow The Sun" on the *Beatles 65* album, already there was a shift and seasoning in the Lennon-McCartney writing chemistry. From the high voltage of the first five releases in 1964, to the sixth release in December of 1964, The Beatles had introduced a thoughtful and introverted side to themselves. And here is where I dived into the emotional well of romanticism and yearning. Forged by their incredible gifts of being able to articulate this deeper landscape, I felt invited into, yet, a deeper part of myself.

My entire childhood was sound-tracked by the music of Frank Sinatra and Tony Bennett filling every corner of our house. My dad was somewhat stunted in his ability to express emotion forever leaving my mother wanting more feeling and emotion from him. As a boy, *his* father had left him and his two brothers to fend for themselves in New York's Lower East Side. My father learned about love from the streets. But, he could communicate his feelings through the songs that he loved. Perhaps a poor-man's excuse for the real thing, it made him happy and it was *his* way. Personally, I think it made him charming. He used to soft-shoe around the house like a kid singing his favorite songs when I was growing up. "East of the Sun and West of the Moon". That, or any Frank Sinatra song with a shuffle feel, would do. According to my mother, he had never told her he loved her. Yet, my experience was quite different. I clearly remember him *singing* to her that he loved her almost every day. I remember the lyrics clearly: "I love you; I love you is all that I can say...". He expressed himself succinctly within the songs he sang while he danced. People would often tell me, later in life, that I expressed myself so much more better in song than in conversation. So much so, that I didn't seem like the same person to them. The 1970's and 1980's were the decades of the "mix tape". A guy might give a girl a cassette with all of his favorite songs on it announcing: "This is how I feel about you." But really, this meant: "The feelings in these songs express emotion so much better than I am able." In the same way that Sinatra gave voice to my father's deepest feelings, The Beatles gave voice to a growing lexicon of feelings in my own life. The Beatles' catalog, in effect, became one enormous "mix tape" of my emotional world.

When my parents were out of the house, The Beatles replaced Sinatra on the stereo. And, that's where I learned the language of love and emotion. The Beatles were innovative enough to capture my devotion and the attention of absolutely every one of my friends. They tuned in to us. They were one of us. They wrote songs for us. They showed me how to love; to yearn and to romanticize.

And Then Came High School

Many of the students at Hollywood High School seemed awkward and many were just plain acting weird. It was a place where the bad boys got the good girls. Many of my female class-mates, formerly friends, suddenly had attitudes or they were guarded and not as friendly. It was where those with the polished exteriors were most popular and the unpolished of us huddled together in Math or Science club. It would have been downright comical if it wasn't for the fact that I took the whole thing so damned seriously. The classes were impossibly hard for me to comprehend. And, how on Earth, would I ever use this stuff in *my* life? Subjects like Geometry, Algebra and History seemed to have little applicability in my present and future life. I knew I'd end up doing something that had little or nothing to do with what I was learning. And, to date, I have rarely needed to use a single thing I learned in High School other than how life imitates the various social pecking orders in High School. There were the popular kids. The political ones. The clowns. The narcissists. The brains. The beauty queens. The misfits. The artists. The worker bees. The poor ones, the rich ones. It's funny just how early on we already had been assigned, and resigned, to our roles — in life.

However, what I wanted to learn about wasn't offered in school. I wanted to learn all about love. How to get and keep love. How to express love and how to express what I was feeling. I wanted to learn about how to be completely, uniquely and courageously — myself.

Then came *Beatles VI*.

The disembodied floating heads from that *Meet the Beatles* album were, now, fully attached to their bodies and elegantly dressed. They had, by this point, become expert in their craft. Songs like "Every Little Thing", and "Yes It Is" filled this heart of mine with such a fierce longing for that perfect love that I could barely think of anything else. Would I see it in her eyes? Would we meet at school, or on my walk back home to the Hollywood Hills? Or on the school bus? I felt the ache for love and completeness, probably, just like The Beatles. Focusing on Geometry was out of the question as long as I was floating on the wistful glances from Monica or Wendy in the classroom. I was love, romance and sex *obsessed*. And, music can do that. It turned on the love switch in my brain and in my body.

And, sure, there may have been more finely crafted melodies and lyrics from Cole Porter or the Gershwin's, but The Beatles' songs had a plaintive cry hidden inside the lyrics. They were doing it like no one else. Taking that step just beyond the sweet simplicity of the Everly's and their divinely perfect songs often sung in parallel thirds. The Beatles resisted the cute, the commercial and the contrived. They steered clear of appealing to audiences and, instead, leaned heavily on their effortless authenticity. Whoever related to their authenticity, was part of their fan base. And since their fan base was, well nearly everyone, I can only guess that there were a whole lot of people seeing the world, or wanting to see the world, the way that they did. The Lennon/McCartney vocal blend, on top of everything else, nailed me to the wall.

Each song on *Meet the Beatles* reminded me of a different girl. "Every Little Thing", though, was about the girl I *wanted* to meet. This single song on *Beatle VI* changed who The Beatles were for me. From underneath the *yeah yeah yeah* of their earlier songs, there emerged a thoughtfulness and softness that was real, vulnerable and completely accessible (certainly, to me).

There is nothing like a song to evoke a time and a place. Listening to "Every Little Thing" while huddled over a Ouija board or day-dreaming in Robin's bedroom, my girlfriend at the time, while her father gardened outside — I can picture it as if it were yesterday. All my friends shared a common love of The Beatles' music too. What it did for our hearts. What it did for our imaginations. What it did for our notions of romance. What it did to drive our sexuality. My teenage emotional world dug deep into these thoughtful and utterly meaningful Beatle tunes. Those feelings united us all. We were all better able to connect and relate to each other using the Beatles' lexicon for connection: Be yourself. Love openly. Be different.

The hours spent listening repeatedly to *Beatle VI* deepened me. I felt like I was being given permission to enter into an emotional portal between two kindred souls. John and Paul became my friends, because I came to know them so well. Ringo's drumming was my heartbeat. As they began exploring deeper psychic terrain in themselves, I followed them — content to allow them to lead. For me, it was as if when Paul would suggest to John to try something new musically, they were inviting me to ride right alongside them.

And, the up-tempo songs had an innocence and electrical charge many of us hadn't heard before too. An unabashed white soul that didn't pretend for a minute to be black-derivative unlike say, the Rolling Stones.

Then came *Help!*

With *Help!*, there was the sense that The Beatles weren't as confident as they were portrayed in Richard Lester's film, *A Hard Day's Night*. Their former confidence could be best summed up in John's cheeky address to the audience, which just so happened to include Queen Elizabeth II "Will the people in the cheaper seats, clap your hands. And for the rest of you, if you'll just rattle your jewelry." The shaken confidence (at least John's shaken confidence) was best summed up with the title song, "Help!". The sense of immortality and over-confidence of their youth began to falter. Similarly, I began to mirror that insecurity. And, that's how terrifically impressionable I was. Picking up on their cues like a dog catching a scent in the air.

I must have looked at the artwork of *Help!* for a long time before ritualistically removing it from its shrink wrap. Four familiar faces looking not-quite-as-cheerful as on their previous LP's. Was there a coded message in the arm positions? "It's just a record for chrissakes. Don't read too much into it," I reminded myself. Once again. The smell of freshly pressed vinyl and the scent of "new" overtakes me like a heady intoxicant. As I withdrew the LP from its sleeve with that characteristic vinyl-to-cardboard sound as air rushed between the two surfaces, I reflected on the hopeless state of my education. My latest experiences of unrequited love. The need to have someone, anyone, see the deeper side of myself. With that, I lovingly placed *Help!* on my turntable.

I was surprised and disappointed by the filler (though excellent) film music stealing time away from The Beatles' own music. The lead song had The Beatles' signature drive and edge. "Help!" sounded very much as if it bubbled up from a stress fracture in Lennon's guarded psyche. The songs, though still top notch, revealed that their boyhood charm and inflated sense of confidence was unsteady, and their former cockiness was now fraying at the edges. Honestly, though, with the amount of recording and touring they did in an astoundingly short amount of time, *anyone* would've questioned what they were doing — and even who they were. Maybe the ground beneath their authenticity was shaken and they didn't even know what "completely themselves" meant anymore. How could they? The group with all the surefootedness and charisma that any pop figures had ever had, suddenly needed "Help!". After all, they were out on a limb, alone, because no one had braved this lonely musical frontier before and they were making it up as they went along.

> *"It was like being in the eye of a hurricane. You'd wake up in a concert and think, Wow, how did I get here?"*
>
> *- John Lennon*

The Beatles only refuge must have been each other. I felt it with them. My first flirtation with, "Who am I, really?" began at the time of *Help!*'s release when I sensed my heroes' wobbling confidence. If I didn't understand what I was learning in school, what did I know? If I couldn't express my feelings other than through pop lyrics, what was I feeling? If I was parroting the ideas of my parents and friends, what were my actual thoughts? These questions started to replace the former certainties. At the tender age of 15, I was staring into the maw of existential vertigo of which the existentialists often spoke.

George's "I Need You" and John's "You're Gonna Lose That Girl" were songs that wove themselves into the fabric of my every day. The people and events of my life were superimposed on the running musical narrative of these infectious melodies. While John, Paul and George were reaching ever deeper into their souls to get to the core of their angst, so was I. Digging into the shadows. With this album, more than those that came before, George took his rightful place as a music composer right alongside John and Paul. He became an equal. As well as their irascible wit and charm, throughout the movie *Help!,* they were now showing a softer underbelly and uncertainty that, once again, made me like them even more. Then, they did it again. They were being authentic even in their vulnerability! As they scrambled for a musical identity, I was sifting through my own shifting teenage identity. Their new musical distinctiveness showed up in ways that I didn't expect. I was stunned at how they re-made themselves. I was surprised at just how much, and how quickly, they had upturned my world. They were only a few years older than I was. How was that possible? They seemed light years ahead of me and my friends, emotionally and intellectually.

I Wanted to Write Stories

No sooner had the band received their MBEs (Most Excellent Order of the British Empire) from the queen of England did they release *Rubber Soul* in December 1965. This was the album that showed the world who The Beatles really were, I think. This singular LP showed me what was missing in my life: An endlessly creative and courageous spirit. The group had resurrected themselves only a few months after the release of *Help!* and they just didn't seem to give a rat's ass about what other people thought of them. They were creating a new genre. They were sticking social commentary into songs. They were songs you couldn't dance to if you tried. These were musical novellas and they were meant to simply be listened to instead. The songs were about reflecting on one's past, a Catholic girl, or a man that was lost and going nowhere in his life. "Isn't he a bit like you and me?" Yes! We're all a little lost. *Yes!* We all see what we want to see. How could they dare defy the music industry and not write songs about love? How could they radicalize the very medium that made them famous? How could they make that leap and have faith that we would jump with them… and still like them? Weren't all songs about love, really? Trying to get it, keep it or get over it?

Rubber Soul changed my life right from the moment I withdrew the LP from its sleeve. Now. *Now*, I wanted to be a songwriter. Now I wanted to be a poet. A creative. A contemplative. I wanted to create stories about the human condition. I wanted to write about my observations of people. The tired and worn-out learning institutions taught old ideas. I wanted original, fresh ideas. Fuck school. Fuck it all. I wanted to recreate my reality from the ground up just like they had done and were continuing to do.

It wasn't, so much, that all their songs were phenomenally good; it was more that they were all phenomenally *different.* And the productions were so rich, innovative and beguiling. I immediately noticed that they'd taken a radical departure from The Beatles' signature driving energetic optimism. There wasn't a trace of that high voltage anywhere on the album. And, I didn't even miss it. There was no rhythmic hand clapping like on "I'll Get You" or "I Want to Hold Your Hand". They were telling us: "Listen to these short stories." The album was so brazen in its departure from everything I knew to be in the rock genre. *Rubber Soul* even inspired Brian Wilson to step further out on a musical and lyrical limb. The Beach Boys' *Pet Sounds* was created out of that creative rivalry. Music had taken such a left turn as to become a collection of musical art pieces on an album that had an insightful angle on our world. A perspective on life. A peek into a person's reality. Why are we doing what we're doing? For me, love songs seemed trite in comparison to the social commentary that The Beatles came out with in *Rubber Soul*. I would listen to these songs over and over trying to get and understand every message, direct or implied. Hundreds of hours were spent decoding every musical and lyrical nuance. My study shifted from the dry world of compulsory High School classes, to the analyzing of Beatle songs. I was an A student in The Beatles' school of life and a quite unremarkable student at Hollywood High.

The colorless world that was shown to me in my school textbooks fell by the wayside in favor of this endlessly colorful musical world. It was igniting parts of my brain that had fallen asleep in High School. I viewed each new Beatles release—and they came fast and furious—as a new lesson. A piece of art, not just a simple collection of songs. And I looked forward to each album like the hungry Sadhu waiting on the next morsel of wisdom from his guru.

Rubber Soul was a perfectly formed gem of a record. It lit up my imagination like a sunrise. It awakened longing in my heart. And that longing was the bittersweet under-scoring to my entire High School experience. Summers on the beach lying next to love-interests Leslie or Vickie. I would watch the sun's prismatic and soft-focus reflection in their hair. I would get lost in the translucent rainbow bubbles of light floating on their lashes. Watch their soft breathing. Revel in the contours of their body and the softness of their skin while my sexual impulses were running wild. These daytime reveries were invariably floating over a Beatles' song. I must have superimposed so much romance on each of these women, where there probably was none. I was refining my art, though. The art that The Beatles showed me: How to observe, be mindful, and record the moment as artfully as possible.

Rubber Soul and *Help!* were their first albums entirely comprised of their own compositions. And that, all by itself, is a statement of their resolve to be true to their musical expression. *Help!* brought them to their knees, and me with them. *Rubber Soul* put them right back on their feet. It made unequivocal their undisputed position in the music world. They had single-handedly transformed the concept of what a recording studio was. No longer a place where singles were simply recorded and produced. The studio was now a musical laboratory where a collection of songs were transformed into slices of conceptual art. And in the tradition of Kerouac, the group had become uncompromising in the creation of their product while being buoyed by the unshakable support of their fan base. Their fans were patrons of these cutting edge artist-inventors. And, I was a fan. I watched this all in amazement knowing that the world was changing before my eyes. Biology, Chemistry, English and Trigonometry simply cowered in the shadows of the Beatles monolith. The Beatles changed my ideas about the life that was expected of me, by my parents and society. Most importantly, I changed my ideas about what I expected from myself. The whole 'doctor or lawyer' expectation was crumbling before my eyes. What was so very wonderful about the professional life? For me? Not one thing.

To make matters worse, many of the teachers at my High School were stunningly disinterested in teaching too. Several, even, were ill-equipped to teach. I vividly recall Ms. Cornell's English class as she drifted off from whatever verb, gerund or modifier she was talking about and began scratching at a mark on her lectern. Sitting at our seats, the whole class looked at each other and wondered, "What the hell…?" Some couldn't contain their laughter. But Ms. Cornell didn't care. She just kept scratching. Then, without warning, she snapped out of her trance, dropped into her body, and began lecturing from where she left off as if nothing had happened.

High School was, at times, just plain silly. The teachers had their very own *Peyton Place* thing going on and the students were discovering their own sexuality in ways that only teenagers can. Experimental and comical. I was no exception. I would've given, well, a Gary Lewis & The Playboys album to have a manual on *How To Be A Gentleman in a Woman's Company*. It was the brazen, drag racing bad boys that seemed to have the stellar luck with the girls though. And it felt like because of the supremely-confident testosterone jerks, I ended up paying for it. "You're just like all men. Men are so insensitive." And what I always felt like saying, though never did: "Well, yeah. If you go out with guys like him, yeah, they're insensitive." I would plot and scheme to meet a heart-throb girl classmate and it would invariably backfire.

I probably should have listened a bit more carefully to The Beatles' lyrics. As a 15-year-old lacking confidence, I couldn't gracefully finesse blending love and sex together. At that age, I doubt that any of us could.

As for learning, I needed something beyond the parochial constraints of High School. There was no class or subject that was going to scratch that itch. No class that would show me how to love better. No class that would inspire me to want to live more fully. No class to show me how to attract a girlfriend. Codified, however, inside The Beatles' music was something I desperately needed. Answers.

The Beatles and their music celebrated their individuality at a time when I was being urged to suppress mine. Their individuality showed up in their interviews, the originality of their sound and their on-screen antics in *A Hard Day's Night*. And I wanted to become more adept at noticing what their music was offering: vitality, humor, pathos, intelligence and insight. Whether John, Paul, George and Ringo were fully aware of this or not is immaterial. They were just being themselves. They were discovering what it was to be youthful, creative and human. They were discovering what it was like to rise at lightning speed from humble beginnings into the world spotlight in a few years. And I, like everyone else that bought their albums, was allowed a front row seat in these personal discoveries of theirs. And their personal discoveries were considerable. Because with the release of *Rubber Soul*, they'd legitimatized songs to be about anything with songs such as "Think for Yourself" and "The Word". They were breaking ground with new musical styles as well. I'd never heard the lush harmonies of "The Word" before. I'd never heard the creative use of musical instruments like the fuzz bass on "Think for Yourself" before. And, clearly, neither had they. I was learning as *they* were learning. Their songs, stretching the boundaries of musical instrumentation beyond their genre (soon to come along *Revolver*) — were reaching deep inside of me.

Deep inside, such that I'd listen to George's "If I Needed Someone", repeatedly, for example, so I could feel what he was feeling when he wrote the song.

Deep inside, so I could understand why the three-part vocal harmony on that same song worked so well, and who was singing which part.

Deep inside, so I could have a better understanding about who I was as this newly inspired self emerged out of the protective—although culturally vital—bubble that was Los Angeles in 1965. But while LA was making fashion statements with jeans, T-shirts and tennis shoes, the Fab Four were making fashion statements, such as those on *Beatle VI,* that I just found irresistible. I also yearned to own a long-sleeve pale-colored shirt like George's on the *Beatle VI* cover, with the white button down collar and cuffs. During this period they all dressed so smartly. I wanted a more English look to my shirts and sweaters as well.

I started keeping a journal so I could get to the bottom of my authentic self. Writing things I no longer felt safe to share with my parents or friends. My attempts at songwriting, though a few of them were inspired musically, fell flat in the lyric department with lines like:

...weeping curtains and my coke has lost its fizz...

No. I wasn't ready for prime time but I was trying. I must have put together 30 or 40 songs at that time. They were all about being rudderless. Loveless. Lost in the great anonymity of the Los Angeles basin. And about endlessly searching.

It was with the release of *Rubber Soul* that I decided that I was padding time with school. I wanted what The Beatles had. I wanted to do what they were doing. One problem. I was 15.

It was a hot smoggy LA summer in 1965. Several things happened in August. While going to summer school, I ran away from home because I had a huge disagreement with my parents. A girlfriend that I was seeing was in the habit of hanging up the phone when she'd call our house and my mother would answer. Not one to be dismissed, my mom let her have it. "You leave my son alone and don't call here anymore!" From my room, I could hear her screaming at someone on the phone and I just knew what was happening. Humiliated, I simply walked out of the living room door. I appeared at my friend Max's house where he and his sister, Bobbie, stowed me away in their attic completely unbeknownst to their single mom. During the weeks that followed, they hoisted food to me in a bucket on a pulley. At the same time, the Watts Riots were in full swing. Dozens of people were killed in the streets. The world was coming apart at the seams. It seemed like LA was burning from the inside out. Even though I continued going to summer school, I kept myself out of range of anyone that knew my family. Several weeks later, I returned home. My parents were glad I was alive, they must have thought I had gotten myself involved in the race riots and had been shot. Several months later and not coincidentally, "We Can Work it Out" was released as a single around the same time as *Rubber Soul*. As always. Their timing — impeccable. Another song with social commentary and another song that was immediately applicable to my life at the time.

Rubber Soul diffused the discord in my family because my attention was fully into the album. All was forgiven, and my parents were just glad to have their first son back. As for me, my attention was glued to *Rubber Soul*. The album defied the very notion of a Beatles 'sound'. There no longer was a Beatles sound. Each song was different. Each song an autonomous piece of an artistic vision of a world as they experienced it. This album began experimenting with truly non-rock and roll themes and unprecedented rock and roll harmonies.

"The Word" was a song about the word love itself. I loved it. There had been so many songs about being in love, but never, that I could recall, about *the word* "Love" as a concept. As a code to live by. This song, for me, echoed the importance of a modern Bible consisting of just one word.

Love.

I felt that the harmonies were, at times, more engaging than those of the Four Freshman or even The Beach Boys. There was an intensity to the way the harmonies were voiced that had the word "new" all over it.

In 1965, when the No.1 song for the year was "Wooly Bully", "The Word" and "Nowhere Man" emerged as something so far beyond anything that had formerly been called rock and roll. I didn't even consider *Rubber Soul* as a rock and roll album I saw its songs as doorways into the future of music. A future where music raised awareness. For me, I was being asked to step up to being a more thoughtful version of myself.

I was desperate to hear the stereo version of each song. Crouching down on our living room floor in front of the left speaker and then on to the right speaker, I strained my ears to hear each harmony. I microscoped Paul's bass line in "Nowhere Man" (on *Yesterday and Today* in the US and *Rubber Soul* in the UK) so I would know every note by heart and be able to play it on a friend's electric bass. Understanding, now, that just like in a symphonic orchestra, bass lines were foundational to the rhythm and lead parts.

Slipped in a month before the release of *Yesterday and Today*, was the single that secured The Beatles, in my mind, as the principal storytellers and critics of our culture. I'd never known music to change the rules of subject, form and production. "Rain" and the B-side, "Paperback Writer", flattened me completely. By then, the band's inventiveness had become well established. They were no longer the four "Mop-Tops", or even musicians. They had transcended the very medium they represented. They were *artists*. Credible and prolific. Like so many other artists that laser-in on a culture's virtues and vices, they held up a mirror for me to inspect my own culture. Ultimately, they held up a mirror for me to see myself. If Kerouac wrote songs, they would've been like "Nowhere Man" or "Rain".

John was responsible for much of "Rain". And he drew heavily on his own life for the inspiration for that lyric. I could just sense this. The beauty of the song lay in how it asked me to examine my own life. Was I hiding from life's sun and rain? Was I living life with a thermostat on my emotions? Was I afraid to live life intensely? Was I keeping my own feelings locked away? Was I an LA kid locked inside of the protected air-conditioned insularity of the LA basin? Was I clueless about the lives of quiet desperation? Clueless about starvation in much of the world? Clueless about the ravages of war? Clueless about the world outside of the United States in the mid-60s? These four young men were stepping outside of their native seaport town in Northern England and were inviting me to do the same. And though Los Angeles and Liverpool were decidedly hubs— Los Angeles, a music, film and TV capital, and Liverpool, a shipping portal to the world, I'd say they were still both insular in their own ways. I was being asked to crack open wide the illusion of the LA egg and venture out. The prospect of that, however, was daunting for a 15-year-old.

Paul had the extraordinary gift at being able to deliver a simple and intimate narrative in songs like "Eleanor Rigby" and, later, "She's Leaving Home".

"Paperback Writer" was another example of this unique writing style. Listening to "Paperback Writer" made me much more conscious of how the bass could literally play off the drums. Paul's inventive bass lines, more like lead guitar lines, wove themselves seamlessly into Ringo's room-to-breathe drumming style. They were just so damned good. I thought they were edgy even though, at this point, they were considered anything but edgy by critics — from what I remember. A few of my bandmates, at the time, felt the Stones were edgy and The Beatles were not. But The Beatles were edgy and cutting edge as far as I was concerned, because they always pushed the boundaries of what was acceptable. And when it became the norm, they pushed it again. They crafted songs that were social commentaries. Though Buffy Sainte Marie's "Universal Soldier", or Bob Dylan's "The Times They Are A-Changin'" were considered more scathing comments on our cultural slumber, it was The Beatles that sandwiched these folk song narratives within the pop genre. And, *by Jimminy*, it worked. Well, it worked for me!

I was a junior in High School. I decided I didn't want to be a loner anymore and began working on having a social life. I started constructing a social mask as president of Ski Club and president of the Varsity Letterman's Club

—when *Revolver* was released. At that time I had created a High School personality and a privately held personality. The High School personality was the guy with a sunny disposition that always had something positive to say. This assured a "friends" base. At the time, having a trusted group of friends was terribly important because being an introvert, as I was, had gotten increasingly lonely. The private personality looked for personal authenticity and attempted to parse through my actual thoughts and feelings as opposed to simply repeating those thoughts of my peers and parents.

In 1966, I fell in love. Hard. But not with a girl.

It was with *Revolver*.

CHAPTER THREE
REVOLVER

I studied the album cover like a research scientist looking through a microscope. This music was — *again!* — a complete departure from anything I'd ever seen or heard. And, again, different from anything The Beatles had ever previously attempted. The artwork was a tame version of psychedelia for the time. Again, like the *Meet the Beatles* album, the cover art was black and white. I'd gaze at it for hours trying to find clues to what the meaning was. I looked for answers as to where life would lead me next. There had to be a clue encrypted in the wild cover art somewhere or a riddle in the lyrics. I wanted to decipher the mystic passages in the vocal and instrumental parts played backwards. Were these guys laying down ciphers at my feet and leaving it to me to decide what the hell it all meant? The Beatles seemed to have all the answers but they would encode them for their fans, hide them between notes, lyrics and album art.

John's "I'm Only Sleeping" and "Tomorrow Never Knows" seemed to be a musical maiden voyage into the existential and alternative worlds of Kerouac and Ginsberg. To me, it felt like he, in particular, was receiving glimpses into the possibility that there was something beyond the visible. Certainly, in any case, something beyond rock and roll. Something beyond this shared reality. Beyond the "she loves you" of the earlier Beatles songs. Even their US release, *Yesterday and Today* (the 'butcher' album cover) showed me that they were really looking to part with their squeaky clean Fab Four image. As they were trying to not to fit in, I was trying to become more acceptable to my peers — trying desperately to fit in.

It didn't take me long to know every detail of those two covers — *Yesterday and Today* and *Revolver*. That was easy for me because at that time, I worked in the record department at the Broadway-Hollywood Department store at the corner of Hollywood & Vine. I would go to the fourth floor after school every day, and the entire summer that followed, dressed in a suit with a name badge.

The Broadway-Hollywood

I poured over all the albums in the department store's bins when no customers were around, usually after 8 pm.

I'd flip through the albums in the bins, with a nimble thumb, much like we scroll through social media feeds now. I'd close the register at 9 pm when it was just me and Mack, a chain smoker in his sixties; he worked in the appliances department. Mack would have me cover for him when he slipped into the bathroom, like a High School kid, for a smoke. Mack would glow when he'd seal a deal on a washing machine or TV. We'd joke around endlessly when the fourth floor was quiet. He didn't give a damn that I was 40-years younger than he. He gave me advice about women and life in general and I would give him my critique on the latest release from The Monkees, Beatles, Animals, Stones, Beach Boys or Turtles. What a fantastic time to be working in the record department! Everything from Matt Monroe to The Kinks. The boundaries of music were being reshaped and redefined more than any time that I could remember. I'd catch Yvonne, who worked in Housewares, looking at me and laughing as I'd alternate a goose step or a Groucho Marx walk around the record bins to entertain myself. The camaraderie between all of us salespeople on the fourth floor made an otherwise boring job fun. Yvonne, while having a very professional on-the-job exterior, had a child-like side to her that loved to laugh and goof off as well. Playful was a good thing to be. Life got so weighty without the possibility of playfulness.

There was that LA sound that used Laurel Canyon as its axis point. Many of my friends lived in Laurel Canyon. Rock artists were common-place. The Mamas & The Papas showed me that, within the rock genre, a Phil Spector-esque wall of vocal sound was possible. There was the Philadelphia sound. The Motown, British, and the American-British sounds too.

Around this time, my High School friend, Kelly once took me to Micky Dolenz's house for a Monkees' tour wrap party one evening. She had been dating their British road manager and had invited me along. Apart from her boyfriend, pretty much everyone else was stoned. Drugs was still a world of which I knew nothing. All styles of clothes were cool. Any way of behaving was cool. Just as long as you were committed to it. Everyone was impossibly thin with long hair and that signature 'I'm OK: You're OK' look of the '60s. With a beatific smile on his face, Micky floated from room to room as he ate a frozen chocolate covered banana. Here at Micky's house, the colorful mix of mellow and very, *very* relaxed people was astonishing to me. Peter and Davy sat on the floor talking to other musicians and friends. I felt like I was at a Beatles party. But this was the LA/Laurel Canyon version. Instead of British friends and musicians surrounding The Beatles as they sang "All You Need is Love", these were The Monkees' friends lying on the floor amid muffled laughter and a low-lying haze of smoke. A few months later, at the Monkees' preview for their new movie, *Head*, where they were all smiles and dressed in white-sequined cowboy outfits, I walked by them star-struck. I wanted to shake their hands, but my girlfriend, Becca, thought that would be gauche. Then again, Becca's mom dated Marlon Brando, so I was outclassed out of the gate. I thought the film itself was very derivative of The Beatles' *Help!* and also didn't quite have that Marx Brothers/Beatles magic. The Monkees tried hard though. Many groups tried, though without success, to have what came effortlessly for The Beatles.

Of course, living in Hollywood as I did, there was always movie and rock-stars walking around everywhere. Literally every celebrity of that period seemed to make their way through Hollywood. I remember seeing The Dave Clark Five walking down "the Boulevard" on a rainy day, The Turtles (Flo and Eddy) on my checkout line where I worked as a supermarket box-boy. Far too many celebrity sightings to mention, but I thought it was like that for everyone, everywhere. But, I was later to find out, that my life was quite different in that way. I ended up crossing paths with a large percentage of the rock world simply because LA was the *center* of this expanding universe. As many of my friends from Southern California now agree, telling people that didn't grow up in Hollywood that you knew this or that star sounded like boasting when in fact, it was just life. Life in Hollywood.

I worked the summer of 1966 as an usher at the Hollywood Bowl. That summer, was a time where concerts hosted many bands on the same bill. One evening that comes to mind was a concert including The Who, James Brown, The Association, and a few others. I can remember Pete Townshend kicking over one of the mic stands, which I later understood was part of his trademark stage theatrics, and at the end of their set, The Who destroyed their perfectly good guitars against their perfectly good amps and all over the perfectly good stage. All I could think was, "What I wouldn't give for a guitar like that…" And I knew there was a sea of boys in the audience my age thinking the same thing. At one point during The Who's performance, I was watching from the wings of the stage. One of the Bowl's stagehands, having never seen anything like this before, was livid with Townshend for abusing the microphone stand. "It's Hollywood Bowl property!" he yelled. As sweat collected on his forehead, he told me he was "…gonna kick that kid's ass!". This band was certainly not The Beatles. "The Beatles were gentlemen last summer," he said. He was ready to go out on to the stage and throttle Townshend, right there in front of the entire audience at the Bowl. He was that worked up and just didn't care. My inner-therapist talked him down, insisting that it must be part of the act and that their manager would pay for everything. Yeah, right.

That same evening, I remember James Brown setting the stage alight. His live, theatrical version of "Please, Please, Please" may have been lost on some in the audience, but for me it was astonishing to watch the master of the genre doing what he did best: milking every bit of soul and drama out of a song. His band opened with a few instrumentals. Looking more closely, I noticed James playing the organ at the back left of the stage. I supposed that it was his way of getting inside of his music and warming himself up.

My younger brother and I were at the unforgettable 1966 summer concert at LA's Dodger Stadium where Bobby Hebb and The Cyrkle opened for The Beatles. In the audience, this time, I felt sorry for the two opening acts, because the 45,000 kids my age just wanted them to finish so they could see their favorite group. Bobby Hebb, singing "Sonny" and The Cyrkle singing "Turn Down Day" were good. They were actually very good and I enjoyed both acts a lot.

Like everyone else, there was a lump in my throat just to be able to see these four guys that had rewritten musical history, so when The Beatles walked across the baseball diamond to the stage, my heart quickened. The deafening screams from a packed stadium triggered a fight or flight response in me. I didn't know whether to sprint out of that stadium or make my way toward the baseball diamond. Sitting was out of the question. But, I sat. And I sat in awe. These guys were clearly in a league by themselves. In spite of what must have been awful acoustics for the band, Paul just seemed to be having the time of his life, his bass lines keeping the liveliness of The Beatles intact. He seemed to carry the energy on stage. My brother, Dan, and I looked at each other knowing that we were witnessing a phenomenon. We were in the middle of a momentous storm of barely audible music and a kind of mass hysteria. This was what all the newspapers talked about. This is what my friends had talked about when they saw The Beatles at the Hollywood Bowl. This was history in the making and I felt a part of something so much larger than myself. Dan, like me, was a huge Beatle fan. Although we could barely hear them above the din, we recognized the songs. The same songs we'd heard a thousand times. We mouthed the lyrics as they sang. And the same four guys we'd seen hundreds of times on album covers, magazine covers and in the news — they were right there. They were right there before our eyes.

On the way home, we took the public bus from downtown Los Angeles to Hollywood. We sat in silence, and in awe, of what we'd seen.

Revolver set itself apart from all of the other previous Beatles albums because there wasn't a single song about love on that record. They were clearly in new territory and I was a willing passenger. I wanted to know about this new musical terrain they were mapping out. They were busting the genre open wide. "Dr. Robert" and "Eleanor Rigby" were portraits, snapshots, of a person's life. They were extraordinarily eloquent slices of ordinary lives artfully portrayed. And, really, it takes a true artist to extract and elevate the extraordinary out of the ordinary. The songs reminded me of the musical storytellers like Jacques Brel. However, unlike Brel, The Beatles allowed their musical novellas to speak for themselves without selling the story through performance or dramatics. I thought to myself, "How the hell will The Beatles do these songs on stage?". The songs themselves had become studio art-pieces rather than concert performance pieces.

Although it came as a disappointment, it was no surprise that The Beatles stopped touring with release of *Revolver*. The announcement left me bereft. They'd found a new home. It wasn't in front of fans with their earsplitting screams where police security was stretched beyond its limits; it was in the serene confines of Abbey Road's controllable inner sanctum. It was peaceful and offered the possibility of infinite creativity. The magic that emerged out of that North London studio rocked my world: Rock songs that you don't dance to. Rock songs that have a message, a purpose. Rock songs with production value well outside of, and beyond, the medium. Rock songs that were reshaping the world of everyone I knew.

The longing that erupted in me with songs like "Here, There and Everywhere" and "For No One" was something I could no longer ignore. Now, at 16-years old, I wanted to write a song or a book about every romantic or chance encounter with a woman. About every new experience. About each place I'd visit. It became a *raison d'etre* that far outpaced the interest I had in any of my favorite classical musical pieces. Songs poured out of me when I sat at the old upright piano in our living room. My parents would often berate me for the dirges I was playing. I wrote songs about Los Angeles and the hopelessness I felt about the place. I wrote songs about the love I thought I could never have. The life I didn't lead. Yes. Sibelius, Debussy and Khachaturian still transported me to dreamy and colorful landscapes in my mind. The dream world I escaped to in my mind lulled me into a reality that stood in sharp contrast to the seeming insensitivity of my culture. This alternate reality that The Beatles had created for me, was at variance with the US bombings along the Ho Chi Minh Trail in Laos and Cambodia. It was a pacifying reminder of a softer place in the face of the Watts Riots and the spread of racial tensions throughout the United States. There was something so utterly end-of-the-world about the war being waged on brown people in South East Asia and the injustices leveled at the African Americans in the inner cities of LA and Chicago. A reminder that amid the chaos, the Beatles were an Island of peace. For me, their vocal harmonies represented social and societal harmony. Music of The Beatles and my favorite classical pieces were keeping me together as the world came apart. To this day, I credit Beatles music with my being able to survive the rockiest, most brutal moments in my teenage years.

Aside from the collision of sentiment with the harsh realities of the mid-60s, *Revolver* more than any other musical statement set the stage for what was to come. I felt it. My friends felt it. And we could all nearly verbalize what form it would take. It was a social revolution. For me, The Beatles were spearheading that social revolution not only with their music, but their ideas publicized in interviews and the political stands they made without apology or retraction.

George's complete departure from the norms of Western music was thrown in my face with "Love You To". A sitar was now made to be an acceptable sound in Western Pop music! The great thing about The Beatles, for me, was that only they could get away with anything. If Gerry and the Pacemakers used a sitar on one of their records, it would've created a whole lot of head scratching. They used their reigning-pop influence to open me up to seeing life as an experimental gambit. This was my first look at the truly exotic world of East Indian music. East Indian philosophy. And, thank goodness, George was actually accorded three cuts on *Revolver*. This was the first time in their history as a band that he was allowed more than two songs. Because "Love You To" was not a song to dance to or even tap my foot to, it just seemed to say, 'Listen to this and think about what it's saying'. Whatever it was that was coming down the cultural pike, though, had to do with this introduction into mysticism. And it, simply, had me at "Hello". Indian mysticism seemed the obvious counter-balance to the material, crazed and very Western, political expressions of the sixties. As was characteristic of The Beatles' influence on my life, I was constantly prodded to go just a bit further in opening my mind. Particularly to having a heightened awareness of the human condition, with all its inconsistencies and perversions. With the spate of assassinations in the US, each new gunshot dashed the hopes of my culture and eroded the dream of the free world. The Beatles offered balance. They offered the same kind of hope that was inspired by John and Bobby Kennedy. The hope for a "dream" emboldened by Martin Luther King Jr. These were angels in our midst laying claim to a world of transparency and equality. And this extreme honesty had begun seating itself in my life. And I loved it. The absurdity in the idea of a "Taxman" and all the other para-social shit going on at the time birthed songs such as "She Said, She Said". The spooky, "Tomorrow Never Knows" even mildly terrified this then 16-year-old. The eerie Lennon-vocal cast against a backdrop of weird tape loops of electronic-sounding seagullls – or something – and a host of sounds being played backward in random appearance was not rock and roll. This wasn't Kansas anymore. This was the portrait of an altered reality painted by four glib Liverpudlians that would just become more popular than Jesus.

CHAPTER FOUR

SGT. PEPPER'S LONELY HEARTS CLUB BAND

And just when I thought I knew where The Beatles were going. Just when I thought I understood the messages tucked away within the wildly renegade *Revolver*. Just when I thought that the next album would be embellishments on *Revolver* with new stories. New insights. Refined musical styles. The Beatles hit me, and everyone I knew, right between the eyes with a concept album that changed not only the world, it changed *me*. And, this time, it was for good.

Was I now to no longer refer to them as The Beatles? Did they have another name. And who the hell was Billy Spears?! And what was with the bright colored satin uniforms? Were they so completely finished with touring and being mop-tops that they were re-inventing themselves as a band from top to bottom? Yeah. The Beatles were doing what they did best. *Challenging reality by changing reality*. And mine was most certainly challenged. I didn't know what to believe anymore. As a senior in High School, there was a tide that swept through my class nearly overnight. And, as far as I could tell, it had most everything to do with the release of *Sgt. Pepper's Lonely Hearts Club Band* in May 1967. The girl I'd been infatuated with, Wendy, and many of her straight-laced intellectual friends, were now getting stoned in the girl's bathroom at school. They would run around the tree wells in the commons area, giggling. There was something afoot and it had something to do with this album. It had a real effect on everyone around me. It seemed to dismantle beliefs and deconstruct cultural ideas that were formerly set in stone. If *Rubber Soul* inspired *Pet Sounds*, *Pet Sounds* inspired *Sgt. Pepper*. And *Sgt. Pepper* inspired the fuck out of me. This landmark concept album laid the groundwork for an unleashing of the cultural and collective mind. I began to doubt everything. Many of my friends did, too. Even the credo of our educational system was on shaky ground: stay in school, study hard, graduate with honors and go to university. If we were to do all of these things, and do them well, we would secure a high paying job and a comfortable future. It was crumbling like my pasted-on smile at lunch time in the quad. The facades of 1967 fell away under the magnifying glass of: *Do I really believe all these things I think I believe?*

Even our Hollywood High School motto – Achieve the Honorable – became laughable. Within the context of an education, what was honorable? Why achieve anything? And, this, was the month before my High School graduation. I'd thought that my future was crystal clear: Go to college to stay out of sight of the draft board. I'd meet a wonderful girl and we'd help each other through university. We would entwine on the couch. We'd have a child or two and I'd go to work while she finished art school and — *bam!* — gone. The dream vanished in a puff of smoke. That month, May, *Sgt. Pepper* blew the lid off what was achievable. Now, all things were possible. This music was so compelling in its Dadaist and off-beat suggestions of reality, that it challenged everything I knew. How propitious, as well. Weeks before graduating, it stirred me up to want more than college, more than a wife, more than children, more than a high-paying job…to be an artist.

During these wild days, I was still working nights at the Broadway-Hollywood department store. The *Sgt. Peppers* album cover would stare at me during every shift. I would stare right back at it. The cover art gave me more to look at than any of their previous albums. Who were all these faces on the cover? I studied the *Sgt.*

Pepper album cover for months. There was so much more to it than met the eye. I dissected every pixel of the album cover. I microscoped every note in every song. What were they trying to tell say? The hallucinatory imagery of "Lucy in the Sky with Diamonds" was at once dreamlike and beautiful. "A Day in the Life"? The ordinary life emerges as something so utterly meaningless, mundane but somehow artful. Was it all a dream? Every last bit of it. The dream of school, work, suffering and elation? I was asking myself, a year after having a relative fix on everything in my life in the eleventh grade, some deep existential questions. The 39 minutes and 36 seconds of this recording had a dramatic effect on unseating my notions of reality. *Sgt. Pepper* loomed as the most compelling expression of art I'd ever known. It did what all truly great art does. It prompted me to be, at once, uncomfortable and curious.

> *"A dream you dream alone is only a dream. A dream you dream together is reality."*
>
> *- John Lennon*

Even Joe, the valedictorian for our graduating class in June of 1967, at the Hollywood Bowl, began his address with Timothy Leary's famous quote, "Tune in, turn on, drop out…". And, he concluded his speech with, "…as for me, I choose not to drop out; that's too easy…" Joe vowed in front of all his cap and gown peers to take the bull by the horns with tried and true American ingenuity. He vowed to meet the demands of higher education and the job market. The rest of the graduates all left the graduation ceremony that afternoon with mixed feelings. Guarded optimism, at best. I most certainly did anyway. I later heard, from mutual friends, that even Joe's certainty about a future rolling out as planned had been shaken to its core. And he was basically doing exactly what he'd so sternly remonstrated against: Dropping out.

But dropping out of the psycho-cultural-American-trance of the sixties became *the* thing to do. It was the accepted. Much to the consternation of businesses everywhere, the next generation of work force was dropping out and off of the production line. For a few years, anyway. The "suits" had to re-group and formulate another workforce strategy. And, hell, it must've worked. Many of the people that I knew that 'dropped out', inadvertently dropped right back 'in' a few years later once they had wives, husbands a job and children.

On the day after graduation, I felt like my classmates and I had been shepherded to the shores of Omaha Beach like cattle in the all-too-temporary amphibious landing crafts of High School. Some of us scattered to the draft-board shelter of "higher education". Others tried to blindly find their ways as artists, vagabonds and alternative life-stylers. Still others were cannon fodder for the Vietnam War, a conflict no one, really, knew anything about. We knew we were fighting for justice. But whose justice and why? Was this really about the spread of Communism and if South Vietnam fell to the North Vietnamese, the rest of South East Asia would fall too? And, the US would have an even larger Red Menace to contend with? *Really?* For me, it was too unclear to be so clear-cut. My parents reasoned with me, when I asked them, that if the spread of Communism was anything like the rapid rise to power by the Nazis for German 'Lebensraum', it needed to be stopped. In reality, we were a scant two decades removed from the horrors of World War II. And, as a country, we were already looking to recreate our glory-through-victory in Korea and now Vietnam? I didn't buy it. For my parents, though, the reality of World War II was still fresh in their minds.

Becca, the object of my affection and obsession for that summer of '67, lived with her mom and sister in the hills above Hollywood Blvd. Her mom's boyfriend, Maurice, asked me: "What do you think of this war…?" I parroted the opinion of my parents to him. He studied me, carefully. Vexed, he pressed another one of my friends, Darryl, who came from a clearly more liberal family than mine, for an answer to the same question. And Maurice got the answer he was looking for. "It's a horrible, terrible and unjust war on innocent people." I was still chasing down my own opinions about everything. It wasn't made crystal clear for me until The Beatles took a stand against the war. As a result, I put on my critical thinking hat and clearly saw the Vietnam War as the most perverse kind of madness. Certainly, all war is madness. But, the inconceivability of that war made itself very clear to me when John spoke out against it.

> *"We went to America a few times and Brian Epstein always tried to waffle on at us about saying nothing about Vietnam. So there came a time when George Harrison and I said 'Listen, when they ask next time, we're going to say we don't like that war and we think they should get right out.' That's what we did."*
>
> *- John Lennon*

Apart from that, I just knew that if I'd been drafted into any part of military service, the deprogramming of boot camp would ruin me. I didn't know much at that time, but that was something I did know. A sergeant barking orders at me would make me want to kill him or cause me to drift into catatonic schizophrenia.

Under the threatening I-Want-You gaze and accusatory pointing finger of Uncle Sam, some would say, I beat a cowardly retreat to college to avoid the draft. The student deferment suited me just fine, though. While I wasn't wild about the prospect of four more years of school, the idea of going to faraway places, meeting new people, and then killing them, held absolutely no allure for me at all. In fact, I found the whole idea of the armed services, going to war, and hunting down strangers with our vastly superior military techno-muscle was its own special kind of bullying. I looked into being a conscientious objector but, in the end, it still served the war effort. I briefly considered burning my draft card. The student deferment offered by my attending college, at least for the time being, was the least objectionable choice.

English Literature was my major, for no other the reason than:

A   I spoke English.

B   I liked books.

So, Lit. was it. The truly interesting stuff was happening in real time outside of school. And it had nothing to do with English or Literature. The history-making cultural events had been put into motion and I wanted to, minimally, observe them. Popular culture was remolding itself by the day. I even remembered Frank Sinatra, that once ultimate purveyor of cool, who always wore a suit and a not-quite-tied tie, wore a Nehru shirt on some

TV variety show (probably his own). The East had truly met the West. And everyone seemed to be modeling themselves after the recently remodeled Beatles. At least, anyway, in terms of fashion and spiritual philosophy. But, it seemed to me to be in the most superficial of ways. Still, it was the best we could do. Even the Rat Pack were fashionable in their East Indian shirts and bell-bottom Beatles pants.

There were flowers in the ring-letted hair of hippies writhing to music only they could hear. Scared boys masqueraded as men wanting to serve their country and learn a trade while they got paid. There were the doctors and lawyers-to-be — pressured by their parents to study hard, climb the professional/corporate ladder and marry well. And, then there was me.

For the previous few years, I had begun suffering from aimlessness and depression. From the time I'd been set free from High School, I was disconsolate. I didn't know where to go; what to do and why I was still in LA doing the same old stuff — working odd jobs, going to school and composing dirges, hunched over the piano. At that time, there wasn't much anyone could do about depression. It was simply a deep sadness that would pass in time. I think, though, there was a lot of depression back then. It just wasn't discussed. I saw the depression as playing a part in a personality split. Some days I was higher than a kite. And some days I was disconsolate with a sense of doom and hopelessness. The real crazy-making aspect to that duality was that the two personalities were irreconcilable. The depressive side resented the optimistic personality for being shallow. And the optimistic personality disdained the depressive for being so morose.

The Beatles had just about pieced my fractured mind back together, but they had also left me to fend for myself. *Sgt. Pepper's* left me no choice. I needed to be an artist. I couldn't do anything that would have earned my parent's approval. Anything corporate or in government service. Yet, there was something attractively sane about taking on a career that was based in self-expression rather corporate expression.

Several months after graduating High School in late November 1967 *Magical Mystery Tour* was released. It gave me, yet, another morsel of sanity amid the chaos of a world gone crazy with the US's escalated involvement in the Vietnam war and the Tet Offensive in January 1968. Interestingly though, even the *Magical Mystery Tour* cover art was a bit insane.

Paul's storytelling in "The Fool On The Hill" pointed to another reality. A grounded reality. It suggested that there could be an island of peace in a restless sea of chaos. Largely borrowing, I'd imagine, from George's new spiritual direction and their involvement with the

Maharishi in Rishikesh, The Beatles were now emerging as mystic trend-setters. Paul again incorporated his exceptional artistry with his vignette of a person's life and as such "The Fool On The Hill" was the standout for me on that album. At once, dreamy, haunting and wise, it suggested that a refuge was possible. Not unlike The Beach Boys' "In My Room", the song pointed out the serenity that exists in an inner sanctuary. The way I read into "Fool On The Hill" and "In My Room" was that, on the stage of all this cultural madness, there was a place I could go. There is a place where the existential angst, the personal demons and the madness of 'endless war' melted away. There was a place for me to refuel; to balance and to center. At that time, I'd begun reading Hermann Hesse, Fyodor Dostoevsky and Thomas Mann. They all seemed to focus on the misfit and outcast that curiously found shelter in his art while the world was cascading in ruins all around him. The sanctity of quiet contemplation was a necessary tool for me in the middle of the cultural vertigo of the time. The Beatles, the European existential writers and the contemplatives of the period, guided me away from the culture I could not comprehend and a military policy I understood even less.

While Paul, for the most part, kept to his very musical and heart-stirring compositions, George jumped in with both feet and down the rabbit hole with "Blue Jay Way". He pointed out that while all these minds had been freed, they were still very lost, misdirected and unfree. I couldn't have agreed more. In retrospect, while I realize this was a very powerful time to be alive, I felt more the observer than the participant. I skirted the periphery of this new pop culture. I didn't participate in the anti-war rallies, though I'd become deeply opposed to the Vietnam War. I didn't get stoned, or dance in parks, or dive into orgies (though I probably wanted to but didn't know how, exactly, to get invited to one) or drop acid. My own overly active imagination was all I could handle. And, I barely was able to do that.

John's "Strawberry Fields Forever" and "I Am the Walrus" were likely the biggest and most influential cuts off *Magical Mystery Tour*. Influential because they were so very different than anything else on the music charts at that time. They were to music what Picasso was to art. Both Lennon and Picasso skirted the outer fringes of cultural acceptability. They were both telling me:

'OK. There is this accepted reality, but this is my reality. And, this is how I see this accepted cultural reality of yours..'

Essentially, songs such as "Strawberry Fields" made me look at the music medium through kaleidoscope glasses. And like the Dada expressions of Dali and Buñuel, I was made to feel even a little uncomfortable listening to songs like "Strawberry Fields". As in Buñuel's *Le Chien*

Andalou, I was the unwitting observer of a straight razor being pulled along an eyeball, I was never sure what I was experiencing with Lennon's surrealism. His songs were distinctly different from Paul's and they constantly challenged my beliefs. Each of The Beatles were breaking new ground in very much their own singular ways.

But, the piece-de-resistance on that album could only be "All You Need Is Love". War, racial division, famine, and disease are the weirdest of by-products in this life, and on this planet. But… all you *need* is love! The search is over. Find the love in yourself, the song suggests. Love is all you need! Stop the foolishness. The negative thoughts. The gallivanting. Just stop. It's all been done before and you don't have to prove anything to anyone. Because all you needed was love. All *I* needed was love. I couldn't find fault with that. I think we all were left feeling good about love. Love as a concept and frontier. Love as the glue that unites us all. Love was missing and *needed* to be found again. But, if I only need love, how do I find it? And, thus, Pandora's box was thrust open. Where is the friggin' love? Was it in the arms of a woman? Was it deep in a remote Himalayan cave? Or was it in the joy of creating art?

CHAPTER FIVE

THE WHITE ALBUM

At age 18, I knew I didn't want to be a doctor or lawyer, much to the dismay and disapproval of my parents. I stumbled through the first two years of college paying more attention to the beautiful and mysterious female students and less attention to what lay between the covers of my textbooks. As 1968 rolled around, Paul's "I Will" and "Mother Nature's Son", from The Beatles' *The White Album*) drifted across my mind like a distant dream. My studies floated on the backdrop of that *White Album* as well as a few of The Beach Boy songs that had emerged from the widely regarded creative genius of Brian Wilson. The Beach Boys' "Don't Worry Baby" and Paul's "I Will" buoyed me up through Astronomy and English Literature. *The White Album*, with its lack of any cover art, haunted me like a ghost. I'd heard that it was a double album. When I bought it, low and behold, it was a double album. There were over thirty songs! I stuck my nose between the two covers. It was *already* an immersive experience.

Having quit my job in the record department, I was now delivering fried chicken in Hollywood at night. And that's a story all by itself! My Volkswagen had the stale carnival smell of fried chicken grease which became impossible to get rid of. Any dates I had would require the explanation that it wasn't me that had stepped out of the deep fryer, it was the fried chicken I had delivered hours before.

The White Album felt like a rag tag assembly of finished and unfinished masterpieces floating over my head like a cloud. The record offered up a diverse collection of songs. "Wild Honey Pie", which was Paul's screwing-around-version of "Honey Pie". Why did he do it? Because he was Paul McCartney and he could. Lennon's "Glass Onion" teased his listeners for trying to make sense of codified Beatles lyrics: "…and here's another clue for you all. The walrus was Paul," John sang. And I was one of those sniffing for clues. I felt embarrassed by this lyric. John knew something I didn't. Didn't he? Or was he just spewing nonsensical lyrics at me and chortling as we, or I, scrambled to make sense of it. "Sexy Sadie", and "Cry Baby Cry" were also examples of this. The lyrics were so personal that they no longer were accessible to their listeners. So many of the lyrical references were directed to The Beatles' own inner circle. The productions sure sounded great, but it was anyone's guess as to what they were talking about! For me, this secrecy heightened the mystery of The Beatles. The songs were so hip and compelling in their *feel* that I just assumed that they must have had a deeper meaning. For me, the *White Album* was a subtle message that I should get a life and not take their lyrics, or life, too seriously. The album was their way of distancing themselves from their own legend, I thought. Without reading too much into it – though obviously I have, and did – I think the group was politely saying that they no longer cared what we, their fans, thought of them. Sometimes, it wasn't even all that polite either. They seemed to be contracting at a time when I was needing their guidance most.

This double album, however, included some of their most beautiful melodies. "Mother Nature's Son", "I Will", George's unbelievable "While My Guitar Gently Weeps", and John's "Julia". They were wistfully evocative of another place. Another time, even. These experimental art pieces, though light and airy at first blush, really did come from a deep psychic ocean within each of them. The songs burrowed inside me. The ballads were more trenchant and passionate than the watertight "And I Love Her" or "Yesterday". John exposed his sensitive underbelly with "Julia" by daydreaming about his mother. I wanted to cry with him and for him. His longing was so deep and so pure. "Julia" would be the prelude to the primal scream of "Mother" which would appear on Lennon's *Plastic Ono Band* a few years later. John, it was now clear, was severely traumatized. I believe that this was the common ground Paul and John both shared. They were both Neverland's Lost Boys. They were able to quell the gnawing sense of loss and madness through the creative distraction of writing music. This was also a terrain I understood fairly well, myself. At the time, I could very much relate to the 'lost boy'. I was a lost boy. And I was in search of a Wendy to read to me. A Wendy to soften the restlessness. A Wendy I could call my friend and confidant. Most of my other friends were sure of themselves and I couldn't figure out why I was so insecure. This is where The Beatles fixed a hole in me. Like the existential writers whose books I greedily consumed like a diver with the bends needs oxygen, The Beatles offered a comfort that was not to be found in my family or among my peers.

Paul's sweet and understated "Mother Nature's Son" was the lyrical equivalent of a Monet painting. Several years later, I'd hear John Denver tell his concert audience at a Windstar performance in Aspen, that he wished he'd written that song and was actually vexed that he hadn't. John Denver knew that songs were hanging there in the ether waiting to be plucked by a composer that could claim it as his/her own. Several years later, in the 90's, I would work with John and came to know the largeness of his heart. He was truly the world's first songwriter holding up our environment for all to notice, appreciate and protect. George's "Long, Long, Long" was brimming with so much yearning that it edged closely to disturbing. All in all, the *White Album* represented a compendium of extremely diverse emotions and music styles. The light. The dark. The silly. The serious. They pushed and prodded me, yet again, out of my conventional beliefs. They were the gurus that constantly joked with the oh-so-serious adherent, to burn his ego and his beliefs so that the real person inside could slowly be birthed. So that the seeker gives up seeking and surrenders the personality out of sheer exhaustion.

While The Beatles were continuing to use Abbey Road as their laboratory, for me this studio seemed like The Beatles' own personal dream factory. There, they produced a huge collection of wildly different songs. Some of the 'songs' on *The White Album* were downright nightmarish, such as the dystopic "Revolution #9". That song (?) scared me then and it still scares me today! This macabre unraveling of our society in a sinister Dadaist jumble of sounds and voices played backwards and randomly spoken words challenged the bedrock of my already tenuous sanity.

From High School graduation onward, I had a slippery relationship with mental stability. Here, I was trying to get a grip on what my perceived reality actually was, and then they threw "Revolution #9" at me! These musicians, that I so adored, pushed me too far with this track. I'm sure this was even their intention — that we would all silently intone, "what the actual fuck?!"

Then, to follow "Revolution #9" with the equally frightening and impossibly saccharin "Goodnight", sung by Ringo. Whoa! The group was bending my mind beyond breaking point. Songs such as those, were eerily prescient of all the weird stuff that would be happening throughout the seventies. *The White Album* helped push the envelope in many ways, culturally, and it helped create a fertile landscape that encouraged comedy acts like Monty Python's Flying Circus to emerge on British/American TV a few months later. And, of course, "Helter Skelter" would be used, loosely, for the justification in Charles Manson's August 1969 psychotic killing spree. The *White Album* was the quintessence of the motto 'Everything is possible'. Nothing is too strange. Nothing is too jarring or inappropriate. If you think it or feel it—express it! And though I wasn't taking LSD, or smoking pot, the music of that year made me feel like I was. The lines between reality and fantasy became blurred and challenging.

The boundaries kept widening. The goal posts kept moving. While I was trying to understand the vision of these seers, I was no closer to getting it than I was after listening *to Sgt. Pepper* 1000 times. They challenged the bedrock of my understanding and musical sensibilities. I always thought that songs, like art on a canvas, expressed emotion better than anything any of us could articulate.

Like me, there was a sea of other faithful followers hanging on their every word. And, they'd make fun of us for abandoning our own wisdom in exchange for theirs. Even "Back in the USSR" seemed to me to be poking fun at the parochial Southern California beach lifestyle. Maybe that wasn't Paul's intent at writing the song but it did point out that perhaps Southern California wasn't the only place to be. Yet, another prod and poke to get me stepping out of my comfort zone and onto the psychic road less traveled. The Beatles encouraged their listeners to become more authentic and honest. This stripped down aspect became John's calling card with a song like: "Everybody's Got Something to Hide Except Me and My Monkey".

The White Album was a tabula rasa with a "You Are Here" written, in disappearing ink on the cover.

CHAPTER SIX

HE'S LEAVING HOME

Abbey Road was released in September 1969. The band was patently out of the box and so was I. But I felt like a caged lion living at my parents' house. Though I couldn't quite cut the cord, I must have subconsciously set up a scenario that would get me kicked out. I told my parents at dinner of my intention to hop a freight train with a neighbor of mine and go from Los Angeles to Seattle. This sounded like a very bad idea to them. They figured I had a rendezvous with the very dregs of society and they didn't want be around to witness the 'splat' when I hit bottom. And they certainly didn't want it reflecting on them. I'd quit all my jobs and applied to several universities, and was rejected by all of them except one. That was in San Jose, California. Instead of waiting for my last rejection letter, I thought a freight train ride seemed like a suitable alternative. "If you take this freight train tonight, consider this your last supper.

And, from this day forward, you are no longer our son," I remember them saying.

And so it was.

With little more than a 'good riddance', I was disowned. It was a relief and a shock. I was far from being the perfect obedient son and they hadn't a clue what to do with me. But I couldn't have predicted it coming to such an abrupt end. Within hours I'd been put on a bus to San Jose. The hope was that I might be accepted by the school there. Maybe they accepted dreamers with ordinary grade point averages.

I fidgeted on the bus the whole night. The bus groaned as it pulled into each of the bus stations along the way. Santa Barbara. San Luis Obispo. Salinas. The glare of the bus terminal lights flooded onto my face leaned up against the Greyhound bus window.

You. You failed your parents. YOU heard me.

I arrived in San Jose early the next morning.

Because I only had only $20 to my name, I bunked in San Jose's Salvation Army for four months with other homeless souls. It was an experience that helped me see the world around me — differently. I experienced how the other half lived (in California, anyway). They were all overly sensitive misfits just like me! I found my tribe, and they were derelicts. Society's disposable unmentionables. There was an artfulness to the way they lived. They lived each day moment-to-moment, and day-to-day. Most all of them chose alcohol to ease, and forget, their pain. And what was the pain? Many of them had lost a loved one. Many, down on their luck. Most all of them were just too damned sensitive to cope in a world gone crazy. There were Dostoevskys, Hemingways and Sartres among them. Some voracious readers, like me. Some dreamers, like me. Many, had a sadness that was buried way down deep. Between the furrows etched in the brow was once a lost boy. A lost boy like me. Like Lennon. Like McCartney. Was this my fate, too? Was I a hair's breath from the life derelict? Was this the last stop for the sensitive male not wanting to kill people in South East Asia or work in a law office?

To make money I worked a series of odd jobs, hanging advertisements on door knobs or fruit-picking. Standing in line each evening waiting to reclaim my bed at the Salvation Army, I often pushed back the tears so that the other guys wouldn't see that I hadn't toughened up yet.

After several months, I had saved enough money to rent a small apartment in San Jose. My friend, George, in LA, had brought me a reel-to-reel tape recorder that had *Abbey Road* on one of the reels. The days of listening to new Beatles' releases in the comfort of my parents' home were a far-away memory. I shared my apartment with cockroaches that were just as hungry as I was. They were so relentless, that I just learned to live with them. Unlike LA's year around pleasant weather, the cold and rain of San Jose in Autumn matched the feelings of doom and desolation that brewed inside me. Again, it was a Beatles recording that offered up solace and comfort.

My first experience of the real world was not as friendly as I'd thought it might be. Maybe I needed more than just love? And I suspected The Beatles felt the same. Fascinating, really, that the cut beginning on side one was "Come Together". John tuned into it. Although the song was originally written for Timothy Leary's campaign for California governor, it felt like a rallying call. A call to free the mind and join forces. But, at that time, freeing my mind was not an issue. Was I any closer to the peace of which they sang in "All You Need is Love"? No. I was desperately feeling the need to be in the company of like-minded folk. And not those united in a cause or a rebellion. I looked for those that shared the same existential twitchiness of the time. "Come Together", for all its hip bass lines and drum fills was still Beatle-esque. The meaning of the lyrics were obvious only to them. The song 'felt' good though. Between the lines, however, I felt that it was a plea for solidarity in achieving more harmony in the world. Here's this guy and his woman addressing all these people lost in their separate narcissist trips — lets drop the masks and "Come Together" and make something peaceful, creative and lasting.

For me, though, *Abbey Road* was all over the place. "Mean Mr. Mustard" and "Her Majesty" were the types of songs I'd come to expect as non-sequiturs after *Sgt. Pepper*. For me, The Beatles' brilliance was in their cohesion. They operated like one person. Now, they'd become fragile and fractured. And the fissures within the group had become too deep. They seemed to be looking for direction in their personal lives through their art. And their art was this finely tuned album that flirted with being a rock musical in its format. Especially the concluding medley "Golden Slumbers", "Carry that Weight" and "The End". Their vocal harmonies never sounded tighter… or better. Particularly on "Because". For anyone who has ever listened to the vocals isolated from that track, it becomes so clear that their distinctive vocal blend was nothing short of ethereal. "Because" was a song that seemed to marvel at the wonder of being alive. And simply being alive was —is— a miracle. "Because" induced a trance state within me. So reassuring. The other-worldly consolation of their voices made the Vietnam War, the cockroaches eating my Rice-a-Roni, and the inner-city race riots disappear…for the duration of the song, at least.

With the summer behind me, I found myself disconsolate and lonely in this unfriendly part of town in San Jose near the tumbledown St. James Park. *Abbey Road* guided me through some of my roughest patches. It assured me, "It's alright…things will turn out OK." I ended up being accepted into San Jose State. The same hopelessness lay before me, however. Though I tried only taking classes that were interesting to me, the school experience was boring as hell. I thought things would be OK if I could just be a Beatle, but how many of my former band-mates thought the same thing? Every guy I knew wanted to be a Beatle. I remember the thrill all my band-mates had just wearing Beatle boots. We just felt like a real band wearing the same boots. One of us would stand on stage like John and another like George. The bass player even bought a Hofner look-alike bass like Paul's.

John, Paul, George and Ringo felt like time-travelers: they laid out the future for all of us to follow. With *Abbey Road*, they'd returned from the future to spell out for me what I needed to do to prepare for the vast uncertainty that lay ahead. How could they in any way be one of us? They felt different. They managed to stay ahead of fashion, music and social trends as if they already knew what was coming. How did they know to do what they did? Even now, reviewing some of their old concert footage, they look like they're from another time. And how on Earth did these four young men, bursting on the American scene in the early 1960's with all this vitality, spark and optimism become wise modern sages in just a few short years? I still don't have a clue. One thing is for certain: They were far different than any other performers out there. They seemed to dust off the time-traveler stardust every time they made an appearance into the present.

The political back drop to *Abbey Road*, however, reminded me of Munch's 'The Scream'. The entire world was on fire, screaming. My personal world reflected 'The Scream' too. Many of the people around me, who at school had 'numbed out', had found the real world was too much for them. Some died in Vietnam. Some died from overdoses. Some died in auto accidents. The rest of them were doing "the work" of protests and political-action meetings. For the other students at school, it seemed too intense for them, at times. With the draft lottery, bombing in Laos and Cambodia, and a limp attempt at troop withdrawal, the Vietnam War didn't appear to be abating anytime soon. The conflict divided the US in very much the same way as the nation is divided today: Those that are for, and against, government foreign (and domestic) policy. David Harris, married to Joan Baez at the time, spoke at my college in LA just before I moved to San Jose. Harris urged all the young males to return their draft cards to the draft board. "They can't arrest all of us," he said. I could hear the exasperation in his voice. It was hard work trying to mobilize a sleeping country — not to speak of slumbering, confused and complacent male college students. It was probably frustrating as hell to put up with the multiple arrests and incarcerations. That stuff frays the edges of the spirit. And, Harris was showing the tell-tale signs. His tall frame hunched forward under the weight of the war. A few thousand of us listened as he explained the power in numbers. His emphatic requests fell on, largely, apathetic ears. Most of us were clueless, head-scratching dumb kids. As Harris left the podium, a guy in the crowd sprung to his feet and yelled, "Doesn't anyone here have any balls?". The guy had a point. I was more confused by Harris' talk than I was impassioned to take action.

The End of the Sixties

The year 1969 was a difficult time. *Abbey Road* was released after The Beatles' final live performance famously on Apple's rooftop earlier that year. On March 15 that year, Washington DC was descended upon by 250,000 Vietnam War protesters. After the first lunar landing and moon walk, in July 1969, the famous festival in Woodstock occurred. Rising global inflation. The Chicago Seven trial. Ted Kennedy's Chappaquiddick Affair. The election of President Nixon. The Tate-

LaBianca murders by the Charles Manson "family". A huge surge in Northern/Southern Ireland violence. And that was only in the West. The world events were coming at me, and everyone else, fast and furious and it seemed surreal to have transitioned from the insular and illusory cocoon of High School to the shock of a most uncertain world of the late 1960s.

Adding to the general surrealism of the whole era was the somewhat flimsy, superficial and tidal quality of the hippie response to the cultural insanity. The hippies' hearts were in the right place. The execution I felt, however, was poor. I could only watch as the bystander I was. Even George Harrison on visiting Haight-Ashbury in August of 1967 said:

> *"I went there expecting it to be a brilliant place, with groovy gypsy people making works of art and painting and carvings in little workshops. But it was filled with horrible spotty drop-out kids on drugs, and it turned me right off the scene."*
>
> *- George Harrison*

Even though I was rudderless and insecure at the time because I hadn't the faintest idea who I was or where I was going, I still felt that the hippie-alternative movement was a bit silly. Why did privileged white men and women try to return to some kind of Native

American Utopian simplicity? Back to the land. In many of the misguided attempts, they must have appeared like fish flopping on the shore of a retreating tide to 'actual' Native Americans. I knew there was something more to it all than hippies, communes and getting high. The Beatles had taught me well. Instinctively, I knew the old structures needed to be torn down — but, to be replaced by what? And by what organizing body?

San Jose State was a poor-man's Berkeley. As such, the protest marches and sit-ins lacked a certain fire. They lacked conviction. They lacked a leader and they were largely ineffective. I instead retreated to my favorite writers at that time: Hemingway, Hesse, and the other existential-crazed novelists and essayists grappling with the human condition. Their books offered up more comfort than the prospect of protesting on weekends and getting high. Sure, pot and LSD opened a door for many of the people I knew, but it was so fleeting. LSD scared me. I had no reigns on my imagination as it was. Hallucinations would be all I'd need to send me over the edge. The few times I tried pot and either saw my face melting in the mirror or felt like my Gumby legs would not get me to the top of my stairs, was enough. I experienced that kind of stuff plenty of times with my own wild-ass imagination. I didn't need to hallucinate on top of my already barely manageable hallucinations

To sustain the awareness of Huxley's *Doors of Perception*, a lot more discipline was required. Taking a pill was easy. It became clear to me that getting high was more of the sugar high variety. You go up. You come down.

And, then what?

The hippie communes couldn't last. So they didn't. I think they just ran out of stuff to do. Not all communes but most, I think. I was always bowled over by the claim that Woodstock happened with over 400,000 people for three days in the mud and there was no violence. "Annnnd…", I'd think to myself. Is violence that native to our culture that peace becomes anomalous when there are a lot of people in one place for three days. Throw hallucinogens into the mix, and it becomes easier still. A lot of the people at the festival felt that this was a trial run for a peaceful new society. This was a window on a future of peaceful co-existence. A society without war or politicians or government.

The country fairs and music festivals that followed Woodstock operated, seemingly, on much the same principal. 'If we all work together, it can work. Leave egos out of it; work for the common good and it can be beautiful,' they seemed to say. (As long as it's no more than three days…)

When The Beatles experimented with drugs, so too did many of my friends. I often wonder, if The Beatles hadn't made their drug use public, would drugs have come on the American and European scenes as quickly? Were the songs from *Sgt. Pepper* and *The White Album* so suggestive of drug use that we all just got the message? The drug culture, like any culture, had as many good points as it did bad. I think the drug influence, in the US anyway, helped to shape many of the new trains of thought and the philosophies of the late 1960s. It helped redefine boundaries; it seemed to help us question our beliefs. And wars were challenged. The downside? I think it opened the gate to everyone that wanted to 'fit in'.

"It was a scene where if you grew your hair and talked the talk, you fit in."

- Roger Smith,
Charles Manson's parole officer from 1967-68.

I remember feeling annoyed at this interlacing of two sets of people — those sincerely wanting an end to war and wanting a better world — and, those that were just along for the ride with their sights more intent on the drugs and sex part. The Beatles' songs spoke to me. But they also spoke to Charles Manson. An "open mind" is a slippery slope. A bit too slippery for the restless likes of Manson. Manson slipped into a macabre world of his own design that hooked impressionable young men and women. What could have been more harrowing than the persisting media image of the Manson girls: Susan Atkins, Leslie Van Houten and Patricia Krenwinkel walking hand-in-hand as they sang one of Charles' lame-ass songs parading down that terrible hallway outside the courtroom. They were certain that, in their world, they were right and justified in their actions. This was the self-entitled white privilege that I remember annoying the shit out of me even then. They'd carved out their bit of psychic real estate and were completely comfortable with it. Believing in their own ideas with a smug certainty. They were completely unconscious of the possibility that they were pawns in someone else's game. And it was that part of the drug culture that I grew to disdain. And how much of this 'create your own reality' was instigated by The Beatles? For me, The Beatles were saying that I should think for myself and see societal guidelines as suggestions rather than universal law. They never asked us to simply imitate them. I respected that humility about them.

Sure, I tried to act like a hippie, but it lasted for about a week when I felt like a fraud and a fool. Talking, walking and acting like I was stoned was a charade. Grass was not for me. It wasn't my idea of a good time. Charles Manson was inspired by The Beatles just as I was. What we took away from that influence, however, was very different. He imagined "Sexy Sadie", "Little Piggies" and "Helter Skelter" as prophetic. I imagined them as poetic. The Beatles, in so many ways, seemed to bring on the drug culture even more so than Timothy Leary. Why? Because they were the most influential figures of the late 1960s. It wasn't, so much, that they may have been doing drugs and their fans followed their example. It was the mind-blowingly exquisite ways that their music was opening our minds. Drugs happened to accelerate that process a bit. It was a wondrous time of change. I can see that now, but at the time I was too concerned about just keeping it together. Keeping it together was hugely helped, though, just knowing that there were others that felt as I did. Through the music that they created, my isolation became bearable.

American culture at this time was jangled by the way it seemed like two different countries. There were those for and those against a war in South East Asia. Even the popular films of 1969 seemed strangely dissimilar in tone: *The Love Bug*, *Easy Rider* and *Midnight Cowboy*. North America was experiencing the kind of visceral chaos that happens prior to cell division, where all the strands of DNA are looking to reorganize themselves into a new form.

And In The End...

My mentors were going through huge changes in the group and in their personal lives. I was caught in a tide of monumental change myself knowing full well I couldn't sustain being a student in school and living in a country that supported a war that I couldn't morally justify.

Paul had begun dating Linda. John was giving peace a chance with Yoko. And The Beatles seemed to shudder under the weight of this dispersal of energy and the personal betrayals. Allen Klein, the man who would become the short-term caretaker of The Beatles, proved deathly to the Lennon-McCartney partnership. It was no longer the John and Paul engine that drove the tremendous forward motion of the band. The release of Lennon's *Two Virgins* in 1968, where John and Yoko stood naked on the cover upset my mom. I was fascinated by the response it drew from her.

"How does this look to his ex-wife? Is this the kind of thing that is OK with you kids now?" I remembered my mom saying.

"Mom, it's not me and my girlfriend on the cover. It's John Lennon and Yoko Ono!"

John was making a clear statement about who he was becoming. Paul would release his own album *McCartney* in April 1970 and George's *All Things Must*

Pass was released in November of that year. They were no longer The Beatles. They were John Lennon, Paul McCartney, George Harrison and Ringo Starr. They had, finally, gone their own separate ways and I felt suddenly abandoned by my teachers… my friends. They were artists finding their own voices and styles. It was clear they were feeling stunted by being in a group. It was no longer working for them and their fans could sense it. It was apparent to me, for sure. They didn't need to be The Beatles for the money. Consistent in their message since the beginning, they had to be true to themselves.

As the western world was concluding a decade and stepping oh-so-tentatively into the 1970's, *Abbey Road,* for me, was the perfect compliment to that precarious passage. I was mesmerized by that album, particularly side two. At that time, I was reading a book a day. I'd awaken at 4 am and begin reading, *For Whom the Bell Tolls*, for example and finish reading it later that night. Somewhere in the middle, I'd manage to sandwich in a class at San Jose State and another listen to *Abbey Road*. I was in a continuous dream state straddling realities of a novelist's writing about Europe — or listening to the supernal music of *Abbey Road*. Staring at the cover art, I often wondered what they were thinking as they crossed the road in that iconic photograph.

Cycling to class, I often remember feeling disoriented in time and space. I forgot if I was a character in the book I was reading or one of the vocalists on 'Sun King'. Immersing myself completely in another artist's creations had the effect of pulling me out of my reality and into theirs. I'd have to say that the whole Fall semester of 1969 was a reality blur. I was thinking about living and writing in Europe and composing beautiful music. I wanted to compose music that inspired others the way *Abbey Road* had inspired me.

CHAPTER SEVEN

THE BREAKUP & THE BREAK DOWN

With The Beatles breaking up, I became hell bent on moving to Europe. To pay for it, I took a job at a savings and loan company in Los Angeles. With my parents, all was either forgotten or forgiven — I was never clear on which it was. They let me pay for room and board and I re-claimed my old room. I thought I'd work just long enough to buy a one-way ticket to Europe and have enough money to survive on for however long I'd be there. I gave myself four months to make the money I'd need. A week before my flight to London, I saw my old girlfriend, Becca. Seeing her sent me into such an emotional tailspin that I couldn't stop crying at work. My parents, yet again not knowing what to do with me, took me to LA County Mental Hospital. There, I was cross-examined by three psychiatrists. They decided, because of my extreme fragility, that I'd be best served by seeing a psychiatrist three times a week and remain on Stelazine—an anti-psychotic primarily used to treat schizophrenia—until further notice. I'd been completely focused on my European trip. My calendar at work counted down the days. 43 more days to liberation. 17 more days to liberation. Etc. Nothing was going to stop me. Not three psychiatrists. Not my parents. And not Stelazine.

A few days before my outbound flight, I went to visit a friend of mine in Laurel Canyon. On my way back home, I picked up a hitchhiker named Louise standing in the shadows near the Canyon. She was having a 'bad trip'.

"I need something to get me down. Do you have anything?" Louise asked me, as she sat in the passenger seat of my Volkswagen. She was absently fidgeting with the latch on the glove compartment.

"You mean, like…?"

"…Yeah, any kind of downer. This is really bad. Really bad. Please help me," she pleaded.

I reached over to the glove compartment, gently removing her hand, and pulled out the prescription bottle of Stelazine. I looked at the blue pills I knew I'd never take. I gave her the bottle. I said something ridiculous like, "…take two in the morning and two before bed." Yeah. Right. I hoped she wouldn't take them all at once.

To this day, I hope she didn't. She got out of the car and disappeared down a twisting lane where a streetlight reflected yellow off of her Judy Collins-esque hair. The Judy Collins version of the song "My Father" played softly in my mind as I lingered there at the street corner. She was engulfed by the night. She may have become one of the very many pop culture casualties like those referred to in George Harrison's "Blue Jay Way".

"There's a fog upon LA and my friends have lost their way…"

Even today I often wonder where Louise is. Did she die that night from an overdose? Did she get married and have three kids and move to Des Moines? Did she turn a startup into a Fortune 500 company? I'll never know. I just hope she made it 'home' that night. Where ever home was.

The individual Beatles had outgrown the three-dimensions of The Beatles' box. In my opinion, Mick Jagger, Keith Richards and a hand-full of others, could not sustain a career outside of their former groups. They needed to be identified with their band. As a group, they created magic. As individuals, they didn't seem to have that same electricity. Each of the Beatles were enormously talented and had very different voices and strengths. Many other bands had one member that outshone the rest, but The Beatles' stand-out was in their exceptional individualism. Each of them were totally comfortable on their own. And I'd say they did it very, very well.

During this emotional breakdown period of mine, I observed that each of the distinctly different voices in The Beatles were emerging as parts of myself. The spiritual side, the sentimental side, the socially responsible side, and the laughing-witness. All of those characteristics were begging to be refined and reintegrated. And, in many ways, The Beatles' final released album, *Let It Be*, mirrored the end of a Beatles chapter as it closed a chapter on my youth. For them, as for me, it was a collapse and renewal. It was a time to just let it be.

Let It Be was a suitable underscore for the summer of 1970. I fled psychiatric treatment in LA and the draft board's insatiable maw to the uncertainty and adventure on another continent. The California life I knew was a dream that ended with a surreal transatlantic flight. The Beatles were in the process of splitting up and so were my insides. No sooner had I arrived in London in early July of 1970, did I head south through France towards Spain. Keeping to country roads and hitch-hiking, I'd entertain myself by singing songs from Paul Simon, Harry Nilsson and The Beatles. No cars? No problem. I'd look at the trees arching overhead and sing Paul Simon's "The Boxer" or Dusty Springfield's "You Don't Have to Say You Love Me" as I walked. My brain was like a jukebox. There were hundreds of songs in there. There was an enormous comfort in being able to have music wherever I went. I'd even get emotional and tear up at times. McCartney's "I Will" was one of my favorites.

I hitched around Europe for nearly two years immediately following the release of *Let It Be*. The album followed me around like an old friend. The Beatles had released me from their tutelage just as they'd released each other from the band. I was now a wandering and crazed disciple of the music that The Beatles had imprinted on me. Now, though, I wasn't waiting on the next Beatles album, I was waiting on the next John, Paul or George album. John, Paul, George and Ringo had set sail on their own careers.

I had no idea where this next phase would take me. I would hitch from one European town to the next, always walking the length of the city with my backpack hoping to catch a ride on the outskirts of the city. I slept in youth hostels, in parks, and along roadsides. I wanted to experience the Europe of Thomas Mann, Hermann Hesse, Henry Miller and Lawrence Durrell. I wanted to know the muse that fueled all of my favorite classical composers. The scenes that inspired the French impressionists. The restaurants where the literati hung out in Paris. The art galleries of Madrid, Paris and Rome. The Beatles' influence persisted, however. Wherever I went, The Beatles were right there with me. In song and in spirit.

Three months into the trip, an older Frenchman whose name I curiously never came to know, picked me up somewhere near Valencia, Spain. I'd just eaten an orange before stepping into his *deux chevaux* (Citroën) when he said, "Most young people smell like they haven't showered. You. You, smell like...like oranges!" Because I smelled like an orange, we instantly became friends. He'd repeat everything he'd read on the sides of restaurants and road signs along the way as if he was narrating our road trip together. He was a colorful guy that would spontaneously erupt into song. And I'd attempt singing along too.

Feeling as if I'd survived Morocco after being on the other side of a wicked case of dysentery, I felt free and victorious. The Frenchman gave me a three-day ride all the way to Geneva. Along the way, we stopped in Barcelona at the house of some friends of his. They were relaxed, and more European than most Spaniards. They were a lively and conversational bunch generously including me when they could. After dinner, one of the group's teenage sons pulled me aside and urgently asked what the lyrics to Harrison's "I, Me, Mine" meant. I explained, as best I could, in French what George was getting at with his song. The Beatles were, again, front and center in this new life. Their songs remained a universal currency; a way to connect with others. Everyone I met in Europe knew of The Beatles and their songs. Their lyrics made their way into the parlance of the time. Dissolving borders. Creating relationships. Translating the lyrics to the song, a deeper meaning occurred to me. Harrison's "I, Me, Mine" had unwittingly become a mantra of mine. I was on a hamster wheel of self-obsession. Who was I, really, outside of the prison of my own personality? Was I no different from others caught inside their narcissistic feedback loop?

While traveling, I had endless time on my hands to think about how the cross-examining of three psychiatrists had summed up my life. case file: Volatile mental state; Prone to treacherous highs and lows. Their conclusion? Running away to Europe was a bad idea. They determined that I was too unstable. What the psychiatrists didn't realize was that my very nature was rebellious. Why would I suddenly listen to the advice of three life-virgins that had never done anything outside of the classroom or outside the sanitized bubble of a mental hospital? My artist heroes were beckoning me to experience life in the raw. I was eager to oblige.

But, hadn't anyone heard? Wars were breaking out everywhere. Traditions were being questioned. The pill had redefined male-female identity roles. Was my breakdown not a reasonable response to a world wrapped in turmoil, and social change? I figured the graduates who went directly to law school out of High School were the ones who needed psychiatric examination. Not me. How could anyone just follow the dictates of a traditional cultural norm in such abnormal and fully surreal times? As depicted in the 1966 pacifist film *King of Hearts,* who are the crazy ones, really? The crazed artists, or the people actively participating in a civilized society at war with itself and with others?

In solitude, I watched sunrises and sunsets — often from breathtaking overlooks. Even though I didn't look the part of a hippie with my short hair and neat appearance, many of the drivers that kindly picked me up would invariably let me know that they normally didn't pick up hitchhikers ever since the news of Charles Manson swept Europe. They said that I "looked normal". I tried, ever so hard, to smile as motorists whizzed by completely ignoring me as I stood on the side of the road in that first summer of 1970. For those picking me up, I was often asked the same questions at some point during the ride: "Where is your family? Why are you traveling alone? How did you get out of the Vietnam War? Aren't you lonely? What did you think of Charles Manson?"

Most Europeans were completely mystified and a little concerned by this 20-year-old vagabond sitting in their car. I seemed normal enough. Generally, I'd guess, people saw me as a great curiosity and there may have even been a little pity thrown in there for good measure.

I was one of many, I assured people who asked. I wasn't alone. I met several like-minded solo travelers attempting to make sense of what had just happened in the 1960s. The floodgates were open. Our minds were liberated. There was free love. Free thought. And, I was free to move about and go anywhere I pleased. There were no filters on creative expression. And, now what? Really. Now, what? I still felt completely lost and at odds with my culture. I was looking for a new place to call home.

I did find some solace. Wherever I went, I always managed to find a piano somewhere. Ah. The familiarity of the piano. The piano that saw me through the darkest of times while living in my parents' home. That funky old upright that my mother refinished with a rust colored stain. The upright that helped show my fingers how to touch white and black keys. It's as if each finger had its own brain and feeling. And I just let them go where they wanted to. There was no technique, lessons, thinking or theory involved. I just let my fingers feel their way around. I let them play.

"Let It Be" was, often, the song that my fingers would find on foreign pianos. The trademark blocked chords intro was too tempting to resist. When others were listening, there would be affirmative head-nodding. Then, when I began singing the anthemic refrain, they would smile broadly in recognition of the melody and at the sound of English. The song itself was the sound of a new generation and a new world. A clarion call, a battle cry, that ushered us into a new decade. Just leave it alone; the ship will right itself. Everything is destroyed and created anew. Chaos is life. And vice-versa.

Let It Be

It was the song that became the entryway to the new decade. A decade of garage sales and scrapping the old. Floral shirts and fashionably long hair. And guys, like me, fresh out of college having their identity crises in Europe and Asia. We were all going to relax and just witness the unfolding of what was. If I didn't have such an urgent case of "What is going on?", I might've been able to simply relax and watch the social proceedings with a grin on my face. But, I wasn't one of those people. I could only 'Let it be' for brief windows of time. I was not wired to simply let anything be, I had to think about it. I had to get existential about it. And there were more than enough existential writers out there to guide me over the bumps and bends in the road.

On the hitchhiking circuit, it seemed that all of us had one book as a travel companion. We would trade one finished book for another. This is how I came to read all of Thomas Mann, J. D. Salinger and Dostoevsky. This camaraderie, usually lasting no more than 24-hours, became my new family. All of us travelers roaming in different directions and even crossing paths again months later. It was a pilgrimage of our own making and The Beatles' "Across the Universe", and "Let it Be" were songs that represented our vision. The songs that fortified and encouraged us. And by "us", I mean all the hitchhikers and vagabonds I met in that two year period of 1970-71.

In retrospect, it was notable that *Meet the Beatles* was released shortly after JFK was assassinated. Interesting too, that I left High School when *Sgt. Pepper* wreaked psychic havoc on my belief systems in 1967. And, *Let It Be* was released just as I left the US in 1970 for an uncertain life plagued with that universal and eternal question: "Am I crazy?" Or as Paul Gauguin put it:

Where Do We Come From? What Are We? Where Are We Going?

While *Sgt. Pepper* threw all the pieces up into the air and *Let It Be* gently assured that everything is going to be OK (even if it wasn't), "Across the Universe" was a song where Lennon appeared to have made peace with himself. Simply listening to it was a form of meditation for me.

"Across the Universe" with its breezy free-associating lyrics and floating melody, pledged that everything could be totally alright depending entirely on one's resolve to stay tuned-in to the beauty that is all around. I thought if I could stay fixed and focused on the beauty of a cloud passing overhead, that I could hold that peace. I could hold the peace that Lennon sang about. If I could *let it be* long enough to realize that I'm not going to be changing my world or any other world. Peace would install itself in my life — all by itself in its own time.

But, those were just words. And I was impatient.

Most of the time I spent lamenting the love I didn't have. The peace of mind I couldn't manage. My sense of purpose was always just out of reach. It was fine for John and Paul. They had money, love, and purpose. But this lone traveler on a desolate road in southern Morocco felt abandoned and bereft in the wake of the great Beatles *goodbye*. What did I have?

Realistically, I knew their lives were just as fraught with self-doubt and turmoil as mine in the wake of The Beatles' break up given Paul's sense of loss (at losing the closeness of his best mates) and John's descent into drug use. But I wanted a fix. I wanted answers and *they* were nowhere to be found. I was on the road and I was on my own. The Beatles did, however, show me through their very presence that a man, a real man, is not defined by masculinity. A man can be soft, funny, vulnerable, indecisive, inquisitive and creative.

A year on the road came and went.

I found myself in the Welsh countryside listening to French broadcasts on a cheap transistor radio. I needed to hear French again. I made my way back to France. I spent a month in the Paris suburbs while taking a French class with a bunch of Italians, Algerians and Spanish students. Then, I was ready to move again.

I hitched through France, Switzerland, Austria and Yugoslavia. In Greece, I picked an Island from a departure marquee in the Athens port city of Piraeus in early May 1971. I met two German women, Elke and Helene, on the ferry and we'd decided, there and then, to share a cliff-house together in Santorini. Their friend, Antonio, found them this spartan two room house with dirt floors and no furniture built into a cliff. For whatever reason, the stark landscape, ineffably blue sea, and whitewashed houses of Santorini had a stabilizing effect on my psyche. Waking with the sun and going to sleep after it set bathed in a golden glow between other islands languishing on the horizon, rooted me to the earth. And reconnecting with the sun, moon and stars relaxed my restless spirit. Nature was all I needed and not a three-times-a-week shrink issuing elephant doses of anti-psychotics. A whiff of the timeless aspects of life on planet Earth and long early morning walks along the dirt paths twisting down to the sea was, ultimately, what the doctor ordered. Doctor Me.

Elke, with the long brown hair, and I struck up a lively friendship that slowly simmered into something passionate. Looking very much like the actress Ali McGraw in the movie *Love Story,* Elke and I would spend hours walking down to the ocean and along the island's rocky escarpment. Long embraces with Elke in the mid-afternoon sun was what I craved. Greek dancing comically with a scarf in my mouth, my belly stuffed with moussaka and retsina from the local taverna, was what put a lightness back in my step. Real lighthearted joy. With new friends and neighbors. Home grown food and wine. Genuine smiles and laughter. It was the ticket to healing. As soon as the warmth of the Greek sun glowed in my heart, I received a letter from my parents, sent to the island's Poste Restante, that the US draft board had issued me a 4F status. It assured that I would never serve in any war. Ever. The status was based on a cleverly hand-written letter from a doctor I'd met before going to Europe. He assembled various symptoms from my medical history suggesting I had asthma. I had allergies, yes. Asthma, probably not. He knew though, as someone opposed to that war, that the armed services didn't want a combatant writhing on his back, gasping for air, in the midst of a full-blown asthma attack while his platoon was advancing toward the "enemy" in a clearing between rice paddies. That just happened to be where the military drew the line. And, fortunately for me, it was a life-line.

At that point, however, I didn't want to go back to the US. I was enjoying summer. Summer in Santorini. New friends. Swimming in Homer's wine-dark sea. Watching the currents of air stir up patterns on the water's surface from the cliff, above, where I was staying. Striations in the cliff face on the morning walks suggested generations before me. Others come and gone having lived with the same joys and vexations. Doubts and certainties. Probably drinking the same wine. Dancing to the same kind of music. Laughing and smiling for very much the same reasons. All the young Greek men and women discovering love for the first time. Was there a Beatles-like group of musicians that stirred young Greek hearts 2500 years ago? Endless embraces in the mid-afternoon. Ancient philosophers, mathematicians and astronomers from nearby Samos expounding on the meaning of life and reaching the same conclusion as Paul had — *Let it be*. As John had — "Nothing you can do that can't be done."

Everything seemed connected. Even the past, present and future. It all came together with the opening of a lustrous window on the world. I could taste the ancient in the feta. The time-honored in the ouzo. The centuries-old sweetness of the olive. The blissful calm brought about by the fragrant orange blossom. The mournful braying of the donkey. My face was painted by the sun. My muscles toned from swimming. My nerves calmed by Elke's voice. My senses heightened by the entwining of our bodies. We spoke of the house we'd have together. The music we'd listen to. The hikes we'd go on. The dog we would have. We imagined a life together and imagined it in every detail. Life suddenly shown in technicolor. There was the sun. A woman. The sea. And islands as far as I could see.

My teen years growing up with The Beatles' music became a vaporous memory. Memories of a longing. Memories of the longing for love. Paul's stirringly sentimental solo songs like "Junk" and, later, "Dear Friend" tuned right into the softest of places inside of me. Against the backdrop of an endless Greek summer, and olive trees scattered everywhere, these songs kept me on the brink of tears of sadness and tears of joy. The sweetness of the fig. Retsina's bite got under my skin in the same way the bitter-sweetness of Paul's songs did. Whatever Paul was tapping into in his breakup with The Beatles, particularly in the loss of his friendship with John, pulled at me. It pulled at me hard. And no matter how fulfilled I felt, the bittersweet undercurrent of a Beatles breakup still ran beneath the surface.

My five months in Greece did something for me nothing else could have. It put me back together. All the beauty of music, writing and painting in the world fell in the shadow of what nature had done for me — effortlessly. This close ally I had in the sun, earth, moon and sky brought me back to my senses. And my senses seemed to suggest that life is a celebration. Not a tribulation.

I was going to let it be just as it was that summer. Figs. Oranges. Retsina. Stuffed grape leaves. The embrace of a lovely, and loving, woman. I couldn't have asked for more. There was something so utterly timeless about the place. Timeless, such that, all my prior worries and concerns melted under the heat of the mid-day sun. The rugged rocky outcroppings in the island landscape seemed to abrade and shave off the puny obsessions of this small life.

Parts of Santorini, particularly around Oia at the time, were wild and uninhabited. These rugged landscapes were the perfect backdrop for Lennon's song "Love". On our afternoon walks, watching as the sun set, I'd softly sing "Love" to myself. The haiku simplicity of "Love" made it one of the most beautiful songs I'd ever heard. Singing the song against the stark Greek Island seascape was like imagining the sound of windchimes dancing with the wind. It was the perfect musical underscoring to an idle walk toward the sun as it gently sank into the sea between Islands.

When Helene and her boyfriend, Lothar, took their walks together, Lothar would leave his guitar propped in a corner of their room near their sleeping bags. I picked it up and thought, "If The Beatles can do it…". I sat on a white-washed ledge looking at the designs the lazy summer wind made on the water's surface below as Paros and Naxos lounged on the horizon. With my feet dangling 1,000 feet above the sea below, I began composing songs. Songs about the day, the sun, the earth and sea.

The smoldering remains of Santorini's volcano hissed and spat on the small island below. It was a stark reminder and metaphor of the embers left behind in Los Angeles.

As all wondrous summers must come to an end, and because Elke was enrolled in an alternative school in Stuttgart in mid-September, she had to leave. If I wanted to stay with her, I needed to do the same. Hardly speaking a word of German, I applied and was accepted.

She flew to her home near Dusseldorf with her friends Lothar and Helene. I stalked around Athens like a lone animal, missing my friends when I caught a train days later. The train wended its way through Greece's mainland from Athens, through Austria as the air was assailed with a sudden chill. It was the dreaded cold of Autumn's approach. The same morning chill that would signal the beginning of school after a long summer in my youth. A chill that gripped my soul. The damnable chill that signaled the end of long summer days idly spent in the sun and sea air. The light-heartedness of Greece gave way to a heavy-heartedness in Germany as its cold and damp covered me like a dark cloud.

But I had the memory of Greece and I knew that reclaiming that lightness of spirit was still there for the taking. It was in my heart. It was in the collection of songs that underscored my time spent in Santorini's Oia.

Six months later, I would return to the US with the promise to return to Europe after making enough money to live on. Elke and I would live in a house in the woods with a fireplace and we'd listen to classical music gathered up on the couch with our dog.

Alas, that never happened..

Instead, I went into business selling fabric. I fully intended to make enough money to get back to Germany where I'd buy a house with Elke. Elke taught autistic children in Kiel, Germany, using the Rudolph Steiner method. We were to have done that together. Our letters became less and less frequent until the magic of that Greek summer had become a memory. A few years after leaving Germany, I returned to see Elke. We'd changed. She was more of what she'd wanted to be — a patient and caring therapist working with autistic children. I became a salesman. The cabin, the fireplace, the dog and the classical music stayed a dream. A dream that, perhaps, became someone else's. Not mine.

Eventually, I wrote and produced children's songs about being authentic and healing a planet. The songs were influenced by The Beatles. They had imprinted on me. And I carried the torch in my own way.

CHAPTER EIGHT

THE INDIVIDUAL BEATLE VOICES

Even though The Beatles had broken up, they seemed to waste no time in creating formidable solo careers. They repurposed themselves. They became even more profound and soulful. In my case, each of their emerging solo voices represented a distinctively different aspect of myself.

John

Throughout that time in Greece in 1971, several of John's songs haunted me. I don't remember where I was when I first heard "Mother", but I remembered every word of it. It erupted from a place deep within me. In its stark simplicity, it cut to a universal quick. "Mother" redefined music, like the Beatles did, but this time with raw and exposed, visceral, emotion like a musical primal scream. Lennon's *Plastic Ono Band,* released a few months after

Let it Be, seemed to uncover and expose my limbic brain and shake loose the un-shed tears and unexpressed anger. John's songs were sung, not from his voice but, from his nerves or maybe even his stomach. I think he was clearing the table for real love. I was prompted to do the same. In searingly honest daily journal entries, I plumbed the depths of my psyche to clear the decks for something meaningful in my life. Whether the meaning was in a career or a relationship, it didn't matter. It was a purging that needed to happen. And, in whatever way, John made it OK by making an example of himself. He made it OK to push deeper into the psyche. Writing those two-hour daily journal entries would continue into my forties. I credit that daily writing with cracking me open.

What complete and total guidance Lennon was offering me on the heels of the band's break up! It was exactly what I needed. I had been labeled "mentally unstable" by LA psychiatrists with their snap, one-size-fits-all, diagnoses. I retaliated by healing myself *my* way. Nature and The Beatles. The Beatles and nature.

To this day, I'm nearly brought to tears listening to "Love", on the *Plastic Ono* album. Or "Julia" from *The White Album*. The tenderness of the man becomes very clear in songs like those. And, his acerbic wit and brutal put downs emerge as both his armor and his pain.

Paul

I can remember sitting in the loft of the house where I was boarding in Switzerland. In the dead of winter, I listened to his "Another Day" and "Tomorrow" repeatedly until the spirit of the songs grew inside of me. Instead of John, Paul and George singing background vocals, it was Paul and Linda. Paul used this blend to make his productions thrilling. Paul's new sound was a Paul and Linda sound that had an edge totally different from the Paul and John edge. He'd found a new best friend and I, like many other fans of Wings, found it musically exciting.

Within the beauty of these songs from the *McCartney* and *Ram* albums, I came to understand that songs don't have to be complex to be good. They don't have to be overly descriptive or ornate to have depth. They don't need to show me how to feel because the song's simplicity gives me the space to feel it for myself. This is true of any truly great song, in my opinion. Paul, the songwriter, was equally engaging as a singer and producer. I remember seeing him on Ed Sullivan's show singing "Yesterday" With a matter-of-fact directness, he let the song sing *him*. He didn't get in the way of its story with facial expressions to 'indicate' his feelings. I always loved that.

Still in Switzerland, I'd watch as snowflakes softly lit and gathered on the sky light above. As that special pale blue/gray light reflected off of a blanket of snow on the roof, I reviewed many of Paul's songs in my mind. As the dream of summer in Greece faded to memory, I revisited songs like "Here, There And Everywhere" and "I Will".

I would go for several hour long walks into the woods on chilly winter days. There was an exquisiteness to being alone as the cold air made vapor of my breath. The lowing of the cows and the idle lolling of cow bells in the distance clung like a mist to the foothills. Here, I would cycle through the McCartney repertoire. All my favorites. The songs took away whatever sense of loneliness I might have had and replaced it with a deeply familiar comfort.

Paul helped me to be OK with a very romantic notion of love. Love became something that happened with the full heart. And, love was the gateway to family. And family, sanctified in love, was the basis for all things good and whole. Paul helped me to see that romantic love can shift into the different kind of love that keeps a family together. My mother and father, in fact, were married and together for 60 years. Though they may not have always been *in* love with each other, love *did* keep them together.

It was "Maybe I'm Amazed" that established Paul's solo career in my mind. To me, this song, with his driving vocal was clearly about his love for Linda. It was about his respect for her. It was about being in awe of her. And he just did it so damned well! I'd stare at a picture of Paul and Linda and their children and *feel* that he'd found his real home. He found it in family. He found it in the solid firmament of belonging. In truth, I envied him. The, often, bedraggled look he had in the final years with The Beatles was swapped for a glowing new-found McCartney luminescence. To have children with the woman he was in love with and to live in the Scottish countryside. It was a yearning that was so deep, that I could hardly beat back the pain in not having it.

Paul seemed to have made for himself, what for me was, the perfect life. He had a family and was making music with his wife. Most importantly, however, he showed me that it was possible. It was possible to have both worlds: Eternally creating music and joyfully being a part of a family. More than the other three Beatles, Paul held up his home for all to see and sang songs about it. The haunting "Junk" followed me around Europe like my shadow. Its wistful, dreamy strains made their way inside my mind and deepened an already sentimental wanderer.

Paul has left me with the longing for family. A longing that has never left me.

George

Nudged out of the Lennon-McCartney limelight, it was clear to me that this strengthened George's resolve to be a creative talent in his own right. His own way.

For me, there was something elegant in his unassuming genius. George reminded me of how we get cast in roles, early on. Within the band, the youngest Beatle was never quite able to announce himself as an equal — as anything other than the youngest Beatle. On his own, as George Harrison, he was the originator and creator of his own sound.

Through his music and the way he chose to live his later life, George showed me what it was to be deeply rooted in a spiritual practice without wearing spirituality as a name tag. I believe that he *was* his practice. I have found that Thai people, for example, don't need to practice Buddhism because they *are* Buddhism. Buddhism is alive within them. Similarly, George's faith was alive within him.

And while George sung of his connection to the divine, he didn't make himself better, more evolved or more important than others. He was forever the humble servant. Among many other things, George organized the Concert for Bangladesh and financed and produced *Life of Brian* for Monty Python. George exemplified what it is to incorporate a committed spiritual life within the day-to-day. In his case, it was within the life of a very micro-scoped rock star. True to his early reputation, George was the quiet Beatle. This aspect of the quiet contemplative appealed to me greatly. To this day, I try to be a good listener. The one that doesn't need to talk at the dinner table. I try to be the listener. Like the quiet Beatle. Like George.

In April 1996, I had the fortune to meet Louise Harrison, George's sister, in Florida. She was quick to show me pictures of George and Pattie Boyd at the Harrison family home for Christmas and other family events. I was instantly struck by George's look of celebrity. 'Normal' people didn't dress like this. Didn't look like this. He looked so special. So different and distinguished. As a couple, George and Pattie could have waltzed out of the pages of a fashion magazine. Together, Louise and I poured over dozens of family photos with George as a kid, a teen and a Beatle.

Ringo

Ringo's unsung genius was in knowing what and when *not* to play. The songs played him. He gave The Beatle songs room to breathe.

"Octopus' Garden" was Ringo's composition. The Lennon/McCartney/Harrison songwriting magic must have rubbed off on Ringo. The song was a hugely successful part of *Abbey Road*. Ringo's role was as a consistent and measured presence. He kept the music, and the band members, together.

I would often thoughtfully listen to his rhythm choices and the judiciousness with which he chose to insert drum fills. Careful never to drum over a vocal or musical lead line, he seemed to have that rare percussionist's talent to intuit the placement of the silent or un-used beat. This is where his Zen as a drummer became clear and why he was the ideal drummer for The Beatles. He was the original 'less is more' player because, thankfully, he had nothing to prove to anyone. Not unlike Randy Newman's brilliant piano playing when he might use three well-chosen notes in the right hand instead of five, leaving the un-played note or the un-sung lyric to the listener's imagination, the end result is something far more expansive than hitting every beat, voicing every note in a chord or saying everything there is to say in the lyric.

Ringo also released some incredibly great albums after the band's breakup. Set free from his role as 'the drummer of the most famous band in the world', Ringo was able to move into his own spotlight. In Ringo Starr's All Starr Band, he played with many of the best musicians in the business and appeared to have a damn good time doing it.

It was through Ringo that I learned the philosophy that empty space is as important as the things that inhabit space. I learned the art of Zen through Ringo's playing. He showed me how to let the moment breathe. I learned how to brush off drama and laugh off the insignificant — from Ringo.

If there was ever any part of hero worship in my life, it would have certainly been these four. They defined for me a new era of masculinity. They outlined the psychic terrain of the artist. And, it was all done in the unstoppable format of music. Unstoppable because, I seem helpless to keep music out of my life. Helpless to keep the beauty of music from entering directly into my heart. As I would imagine for most us, music bypasses the brain and its filters. And, though The Beatles had likely not done this with intention, their music found its way into my very cells. Their music provided the doorway to deeper learning: visceral and life-learning. And it's even found its way into my unconscious mind as many of the mantra-like strains persist in my daily internal narrative. The Beatles' music gave me the courage to step onto my own path. Use my own voice. And maybe more than all else, it helped me when I'd "find myself in times of trouble".

CHAPTER NINE

ALL I REMEMBER IS THE MUSIC

I found that in my creative voice there was more than music, writing or art. With The Beatles' example, I'd found a way to build a creative *life*. They showed me by example how to think and exist in the world creatively, not just as a survivor or a consumer. They helped me to see that cultural guidelines are constructions. And while guidelines are important to a culture, they can be devastating to the creative individual, as they were devastating to me. Throughout much of my early life, I kept a tight leash on myself by never wanting to step out of bounds so I could be accepted. This need for acceptance often destroyed my natural inclinations for critical and creative thinking:

Wait a minute. I shouldn't think or feel that way! I need to be more acceptable. More like others.

I found that the cultural boundaries and guidelines simply needed to be seen for what they were. Not as absolutes. Not as cement guard-rails. When The Beatles changed the very definition of pop music, they similarly expanded on the idea of the life unfettered by societal constraints. It wasn't just their music. They blew open the myth about needing to be socially acceptable through:

- Their fashion statements
- Their political stands against the Vietnam War
- Their convictions about racial equality when all four of them refused to perform to a segregated audience in Jacksonville, Florida or anywhere for that matter.
- Their stand on drugs, taxation and oppressive government.

In my opinion, The Beatles used their popularity and their celebrity to emotionally and intellectually advance their listeners.

The Beatles, and their music, 'held my hand' as I weathered the nagging reminders that I was utterly and ultimately alone in this world. The Beatles and those existential writers of the 1930's and 1940's — Henry Miller, Sartre, Beauvoir, Camus and, even, Lawrence Durrell — were such a comfort to me. Knowing that I wasn't the only social/emotional cripple and that there were many that were more articulate, courageous and creative than I, came as a tremendous relief to my sanity.

With The Beatles' disbanding, I was on my own. I was on my own to find the same kind of voice inside of me that incited Paul's genius for melody writing. His gift of music production and his penchant for finding and experimenting with new sounds. John's primal scream and political activism. George's incredible and, often, under-appreciated depth and intelligence. Ringo's Zen-like attitude. The four of them found their places in my psyche. Was there another band that had the creative punch as a band or as individuals? For me, there wasn't.

The band inspired authenticity in me, and to the musicians that followed them. They urged their fan base, through recordings, interviews and films to follow their bliss — as Joseph Campbell often talked about. To follow the bliss in the only unique way each of us is able.

Without waiting as eagerly as I once had for each Beatles release, I followed their separate solo musical careers with keen interest. Out of one voice, there were four distinctly different voices. And each of them, curiously, seemed to focus on a different part of the collective human psyche. And if not the human psyche, they certainly focused on different parts of my psyche. Again, by example, they helped shape my life with some of the most important teachings I'd ever learned.

Be authentic and find your own voice.

Create your own reality.

Relax and let it all be what it needs to be.

Oh and, here, let me hold your hand.

Who will hold my hand this time? This time, today, right now, when there is more at stake than simply helping *me* through a rocky adolescence. Who will hold our hands through a *world* rocked by strange weather patterns, viral pandemics and deep political divisiveness and social upheaval?

CHAPTER TEN

ALL YOU NEED IS LOVE

During the calamitous times of the early sixties, it was an appropriate moment for The Beatles to sing, 'I Want To Hold Your Hand'. The grayer than gray days following the Kennedy assassination are strikingly familiar to the surreal-ness of today's rocky political climate.

What I wouldn't give for the modern day equivalent of four young men enthusiastically lifting our hearts in the excitement and freshness of their songs. Instead of teenage girls screaming *en masse*, we would all privately be mouthing: "Yes! This is good. This is right."

I think we all need a Beatles "yeah, yeah, yeah," now.

What form a Beatles invasion would take in the twenty-first century is anyone's guess: a songwriter, performer, blogging sage or viral video? It would have to be something extraordinary that diverted everyone's attention like The Beatles captivated the world more than six decades ago. Will they be time-travelers, extra-terrestrials or a band of impassioned and articulate children united in their voices to campaign for their survival into adulthood? The spirited youthful conviction of a Joan of Arc or Malala Yousafzai to electrify a youthful following and send the old guard, protecting their selfish stakes in a future only for themselves, cowering and fleeing for cover. Or the conviction of a Rosa Parks who simply decided that the regional cultural convention was not *her* convention.

No, the only tired I was, was tired of giving in.

- Rosa Parks

The Beatles, after all, successfully reminded us all that there is power in the prescient voice of youth. Theirs was a youthful voice. They reminded me that there is no force greater than the fresh, the vital, the creative, the passionate. When I hear an impassioned and youthful voice speak out, I hear the voice of a dedicated individual taking what The Beatles laid out to the next level. The Beatles invited me, us, to view life differently. Youthful and adrenalized voices remind me to value and protect life differently — to protect life right now.

But right now. What could turn our heads the way The Beatles did? Something to coax our attention away from the near-sensationalist global news feed, and an enticement away from today's smartphone stupor and binge-watching video addiction. What would it take to lift our heads up?

Yeah, Yeah, Yeah – Yes!

The persistently W-T-F-ness of world events seem to beg for relief. A reprieve. An optimistic footnote. *Anything*.

Could the lives of many millions of people be any more unsettled right now? Yet, down the halls of my memory I hear a reverberate: "Yeah, you, got that something. I think you'll understand. When I, feel that something, *I wanna hold your hand*...." A huge sigh sweeps over me. That sound, that *feeling*, was so innocent and refreshing all those years ago. And yet it was so powerful. The Beatles was an injection of hope when there was little to be found. It was an irresistible invitation to view the world anew. We trusted them. I trusted them.

I knew The Beatles would guide us, tend to us through those somber, bleak November days in '63. In fact, they guided me throughout the treachery of my teenage years.

But to whom can the sensitive teen turn now? I can't know because I am of a different generation, but I was beyond fortunate to have four young men that felt like brothers to me. They helped me through the worst of it. They did it elegantly. And I turned out OK. In the end.

I think the world needs a new vitality that The Beatles offered now more than it did in that bleak month of February 1964 when they burst onto the world stage. I could go for another exciting wide-eyed moment of hope on an Ed Sullivan-type show. I could go for something that has never before been experienced. A prescient individual or individuals capturing the heart and soul of a global community with the promise of a brighter and truly different world. Now, with the Internet, Podcasts and video streaming, I imagine a kind of global *Ed Sullivan Show*. Doing what that appearance in early 1964 did then. But, NOW!

A *Rubber Soul* but for today. Thoughtful, compelling and original. A purposeful step away from the insulated virtual, and predictable, pablum of today. I would love to see people guided to a new way of looking at things. I would love to see a restructuring of outdated beliefs. I would love to see a new world with new ideas bubbling up from the endless reservoir of a youthful and fanciful imagination. What if it were something as bold and as innovative as *Sgt. Pepper's Lonely Hearts*

Club Band? Would it be enough to galvanize and unify us in today's world as it did five decades ago? Would it dispel the darkness and confusion and transform our global community into one of hope, prosperity and unity? Would that jolt be from a new type of music? A new way of transmitting information? A new way of deprogramming the present cultural hypnosis (that doesn't appear to be doing anything for anyone — apart from the ultra-wealthy)?

> *Who would we be today if it had not been for The Beatles yesterday?*
>
> *In what ways would our culture have been poorer if not for The Beatles?*

These may sound like grandiose pronouncements, but the 60's laid the groundwork for where we are today culturally, in my opinion. And The Beatles shaped the 60's in no insignificant way. That group enriched my life by suggesting how I might think creatively. They suggested to me that living outside the box was not only a possibility but a *necessity* particularly for the blossoming creative spirit. Most certainly, I'd be less of a person had it not been for those four guys from Liverpool. And their gift of music keeps on giving every time I play one of their songs again. It *endures* inside the culture and inside my psyche.

And, if another kind of Beatles phenomenon appeared, in what way would our collective spirits be lifted? How would it change our world?

I wait and I wonder.

AFTERWORD

After several attempts at landing recording contracts with major pop record labels, I turned to recording children's music in 1988. On my terms. In my studio. Playing all the instruments. It was deeply satisfying. There was no record label or producer telling me how to do the music. No conflicts with band members. No arguments over who composed what. This was an opportunity for me to be inside the music. And the songs were for children. That wonderfully inspired and creative part of our cultures that many of us believe are in the process of growing — forming into adults. I came to believe that they are fully formed just as they are and, in many ways, a good deal better *in*formed than most adults. And to record music for them that might inspire them just like The Beatles inspired me, well, that's what I wanted to do. I felt privileged to do it. And for the very first time in my life, my purpose was clear. I wanted to be a musical 'catcher in the rye'. Just like The Beatles 'caught' a generation, sparing us from the oh-so-ordinary life if we so chose. I wrote and recorded songs about being authentic, creative and living a life outside the guide lines. And, that our imaginations are the most powerful gifts we have. I was able to sing exactly what was on my mind and in my heart.

As a children's recording artist and entertainer, I was able to meet many other musicians, actors and political speakers.

Remarkably, with all the people I've met in my lifetime: icons like Cat Stevens, Michael Jackson and John Denver, I'd never actually met my mentors: The Beatles. It was enough for me to meet Victor Spinetti several times in my London music publisher's office and to be in the presence of this high-spirited man. Spinetti is a character actor who appeared in all The Beatles' films and, apparently, a close friend of the band. Of Victor, George said, "You've got a lovely karma, Vic." And, Paul described Victor as "The man who makes clouds disappear."

But, in truth, I never needed to actually meet The Beatles. Their songs and their presence live in me. I couldn't have been born in a more dynamic time in our history. And, to have four clever Liverpudlians hold my hand through those most tumultuous and exciting of times, was a huge — plus.

www.ingramcontent.com/pod-product-compliance
Lightning Source LLC
Chambersburg PA
CBHW031947070426
42453CB00007BA/408